CORNISH SEAFARERS

THE SMUGGLING, WRECKING & FISHING LIFE OF CORNWALL

by

A. K. HAMILTON JENKIN
M.A., B.Litt.(Oxon)

With an Introduction by
SIR ARTHUR QUILLER-COUCH

With eight pages of illustrations

Douglas, St. Ives

A Cornish Seafarer

INTRODUCTION

Books about Cornwall have multiplied in my lifetime at an astonishing rate and with gathering volume. In my infancy the railway had scarcely begun to awaken curiosity in this remote, but recently accessible, land and its people: many of whom—and some of them well known to me—lived and died contentedly without ever having set eyes on a locomotive. The arrival of the motor, moderately priced, has swelled the number of guide-books, illustrated books, chatty books for the tourist, little books of legendary stuff (some of it surprisingly well invented), handy folding maps, obliging descriptions of the Cornish, their manners, customs, foibles, eccentricities; almost to a "harmonical progression." While of late a most careful Survey prepared by Mr. W. Harding Thompson for the Council for the Preservation of Rural England, sumptuously printed and illustrated, has not only shown what the many characteristic beauties of Cornwall are, but attempted winningly to teach how they should be preserved from the tooth of Time, rescued from spoiling by commercial greed, and even improved by intelligent planting and planning for the future.

But before all this book-making actively began, lovers of our land—here and there, in sequestered spots and with no prospect of earning a penny by it—

were laboriously collecting, shaping, indexing all records they could lay hold on, by document or tradition, of their chosen corner, its history, its topography, the fauna and flora of the countryside, their neighbours' family traditions, events that now and then excite a village and startle it even into public importance for a while. I pay a small pious debt to the memory of my own grandfather, who happened to be such a man —a naturalist in the line of Gilbert White of Selborne, accurate to observe, faithful to record, setting the result down in the severe English of a man who had trained himself to quiet, scholarly prose. His modest contribution in its kind—"Polperro, its History, etc." —I mention here because, with its documents and records of "natural phenomena," it includes descriptions of his lifelong neighbours, the fishermen, their ways and modes of industry; as also because the book contained a chapter on Privateers and Smugglers from which the late Captain H. N. Shore (afterwards Lord Teignmouth), so often quoted in the following pages, derived much of the material he reproduced in more popular language.

But, for our good fortune, concurrently with this spate of "topical" books about Cornwall there has established itself a quiet group of genuine seekers into her past. The old race of devoted inquirers—the sort of men who founded the Royal Institution of Cornwall —were scattered, worked sporadically. Many of them, like so many local antiquarians, even to-day, were cranks, holding theories about Druids, or intent to prove the Cornish (God forbid!) one of the Lost

INTRODUCTION   vii

Tribes. Given an obsession, and a heated brain working in solitude, there is no telling to what lengths of speculation we may not be carried. But Cornwall to-day has somehow found a group of workers, of whom Mr. A. K. Hamilton Jenkin is among the foremost, who seriously devote themselves to keeping alive an interesting, if almost defunct, language; in reviving the embers of ancient festivities, almost extinct in Cornwall, as, for example, the happy social art of chamber-music lies almost extinct to-day, crushed by the same heat of a mistaken Puritanism; in recapturing (more scientifically to-day than did Bottrell, Hunt, and some others for whose pains we yet give thanks) the racial legends and household tales before they quite fade out—as a last loiterer beside the inn-fire will rise and remove himself into the night.

The race of yore
Who danced our infancy upon their knee
And told our marvelling boyhood legends store
Of their strange ventures happ'd by land or sea,
How are they blotted from the things that be!

But there are other records, less "romantic" perhaps to the superficial mind, perhaps even more evanescent in memory—recollections of the ways, habits, and daily occupations of the Cornish in quite recent generations—which also, to the discerning reader, have the deep import of actual life, with its struggles, anxieties, frequent and astonishing heroism. Beneath a pile of dusty newspaper entries, share-lists, sailings of emigrant ships, etc., or hidden in treasured private letters, must lie the heroic tale of the Cornish "forty-niners," of the shutting-down of work at home, dwindling wage, semi-starvation, sudden hope, decision (at what cost!), the break-up of homes in home-devoted families, the great adventure to Nevada or California. The event of those days in the small port of Fowey, where my home is, would be the arrival or departure of one of its two sailing-brigs: bringing home, in lessening quantity, timber for mine-props, carrying away, in gathering numbers, the Duchy's adventurous youth.

To this tale of the Cornish Miner Mr. Hamilton Jenkin gave his time and toil in a previous book. He here turns an equal care to serve the story of our seafarers and fishermen. I thank him particularly for having, without prejudice or parti pris, reduced the old legend of "wrecking" to history and proportion.

ARTHUR QUILLER-COUCH.

1932.

AUTHOR'S PREFACE

It is not without reason that the Cornish people have always been regarded as a race apart. Even to-day, despite the loss of their native language, they retain, to a surprising degree, the characteristics which mark them still as Celts. It is not only the distance of Cornwall from the great centres of population which has helped to preserve this distinctive character in its inhabitants. The land itself is different from any other English county—a long bony ridge reaching far out by west and south into the immensity of the Atlantic Ocean. Though now becoming known as an English riviera, the essential attributes of Cornwall are in truth the reverse of tropical luxuriance. It was not indeed in the cultivation of its, for the most part, barren surface that the people of Cornwall formerly looked for a return on their labour. The wealth of the Duchy, as they knew it, lay buried deep in the hills of granite, and in the waters which surrounded their cliff-girt home. Hence it was that, in times past, but two forms of occupation lay open to the majority of Cornishmen, and it was by instinct, rather than conscious choice that one generation followed another to the mine or to the boat. The story of the former has been told by the writer in his book, *The Cornish Miner*. The present volume traces the fortunes of those who followed the sea as their calling. It is well to state, however, that this is not a book about great seamen and explorers, the famous westcountrymen of history. Cornwall has had her share of these: Old Dreadnought Boscawen, who fought the Spaniards at Porto Bello; Edward Pellew whose bombardment broke the slave trade of Algiers; Breadfruit Bligh, who accompanied Cook to the southern seas. But behind such men as these there have at all times

AUTHOR'S PREFACE

stood the rank and file of common seafarers, on whose grit and endurance Britain's reputation as a maritime power was built.

The long-shore life of the Cornish fishing coves and ports was a hard school in which such seamen were raised. It was a school which tended to produce much originality of character, and its ethics were all its own. Its products were alike to be seen in the law-evading smuggler, the bandit wrecker, or the poor toiling fisherman. But whilst the parts played by such men were at all times interchangeable, and no strict line of demarcation divided their ranks, one characteristic was common to them all: they were, in very truth, "men of the sea."

The purpose of this book is to relate the story of that sea-life of the past, a story which constitutes one of the most enthralling and significant chapters in the history of the Cornish people, and one which is essential to the understanding of much that survives in Cornwall to-day. More, however, still remains to be told; and in order to complete the picture of every-day life as it was in this once remote and still delectable corner of Celtic Britain, the writer has two further books in preparation. These will deal with the cottage homes, the customs and folk-lore, and above all, with the spirit of fervent devotion which gave backbone and character to the people of "Old Cornwall."

A. K. HAMILTON JENKIN.

St. Ives, Cornwall, 1932.

CONTENTS

	PAGE
INTRODUCTION BY SIR ARTHUR QUILLER-COUCH	v
AUTHOR'S PREFACE	ix

THE SMUGGLERS

Cornishmen and the Sea—Smuggling in Fact and Fiction—Smuggling and Methodism—Records of Violence—Smugglers and the Press-gang—Excisemen's Errors—A Smuggling Tragedy—Smuggling at its Zenith—Reckless Daring—"Cruel" Coppinger—The Honest "Fair Trader"—A Smuggler King—Falmouth Packet Boats—Lawless Privateers—Perils of the Trade—A Royal Pardon—Turning King's Evidence — Crossing from Roscoff — Outwitting the "Sarcher"—The Penalties of Smuggling—Hairbreadth Escapes—The Smugglers' Generosity—"One and All"—An Act of Bravado—A Pauper Funeral—Government Spies—The Last Days of Smuggling 3

WRECKS AND WRECKERS

The Lighter Side of Wrecking—Its Practice in Early Times—The "Right of Wreck"—Loss of a Royal Treasure Ship—Cornish Gentry as Wreckers—The First Lighthouses—"God's Grace" to the Poor—Parson Troutbeck's Prayer—The Wreckers of Mounts Bay—The Wreck of Sir Cloudesley Shovel—Burial of Corpses—Commodore Walker at St. Ives—The Dangers of Going A'Wrecking—Wrecking at its Height—Duping the Excisemen—Beach-combing—"Bo'sun" Smith on Wrecking—The Loss of *The Good Samaritan*—Records of Life-saving—Wreck of the *Anson*—Cornish Bravery—Trengrouse and his Rocket Apparatus—The Profits of Pilotage—Wreck of the *North Britain*—Salute to the Life-boat Service 75

xii   CONTENTS

THE FISHERMAN'S TRADE

The Sailing of the Fleet—"The Price of Fish"—Profits of the Middlemen—Sunday Observance—Fishing in Elizabethan Times—The Newfoundland Trade—Spanish Wars—Cornish Fishermen and Turkish Pirates—The Pilchard Fishery in the Eighteenth Century—Trade with Italy—The Napoleonic Wars—Cornish Fishing at its Hey-day—Huge Catches—The Launching of the Seine Boats—The "Huer" at his Work—The Taking of a Shoal—Night Work in the Fish Cellars—Curious Methods of Payment—"Cellar Feasts"—The Irish Herring Fishery—The End of Seining—Fishing Customs—The Mount's Bay Mackerel Fleet—Mousehole "Yawlers"—Penzance Fishwives—Coming of the Trawler and Steam Drifter—The Newlyn Riot—Decay of the Inshore Fisheries—A Scottish Parallel—Belgian motor-craft—Possibilities of the Future. 137

INDEX 215

LIST OF ILLUSTRATIONS

A Cornish Seafarer	*Frontispiece*
The Smugglers (after Rowlandson) . .	*facing page* 16
"The King of Prussia's" Cove . .	,, 33
Clearing a Wreck in Cornwall (after Rowlandson)	,, 90
"Bulking" Pilchards in a Fish Cellar .	,, 161
A Huer Signalling (with "Bushes" and Trumpet)	,, 176
A Seine of Pilchards	,, 180
An Old Fish "Jouster"	,, 189

THE SMUGGLERS

THE SMUGGLERS

I

THE story of the "long-shore" life of Cornwall, rich as it is in colour, incident, and high romance, has never yet been told in full by any writer, for the very reason perhaps that its many-sidedness and complexity forbid its telling within the limits of any book of ordinary length. Throughout that varied length of coastline, from Hartland Point to the Land's End and onward thence to Plymouth Sound where the dividing waters of the Tamar reach the sea, secluded coves and rocky inlets, frowning cliffs, sandy towans and deep sea-creeks—the latter often biting far inwards upon the bosom of the land—are all rich in the unwritten stories of a population who as smugglers, wreckers, pirates, and fishermen have looked to the sea for their livelihood and support. For it is thus that the Cornishman has ever regarded the waters that surround the far-outstretching promontory which constitutes his home. Living as he does within sight and sound of the sea, he has little in common with the townsman who glorifies it for its beauty or sentimentalizes over its treachery and untamable power. To the Cornishman rather it is a harvest-field from which it is possible to wrest a hard-earned living, sometimes a battle-field upon which he may be called to fight for his very life. In consequence of this he neither dreads nor romantically loves the sea, for he knows it for what it is. Part and parcel of his life, he has seen it in its every mood, conscious all the while that each must be watched and studied if he is to gain the mastery in that never-ending contest wherein man is pitting his intelligence against the forces of nature.

It is, perhaps, only natural that with the passing of time, the realities of a life which is now receding into the background of the past should become overlaid by the imaginative conceptions of a later day. Particularly does this apply to that branch of the old seafaring life of the west which falls under the heading of smuggling. It is true that any one who is sufficiently steeped in the stories of the smugglers and who has visited the coves wherein some of their most daring deeds were enacted, will probably have found it easy to conjure up some not unsatisfactory vision of the past. As the dusk of an autumn evening descends, it is not hard to fancy that one sees again the rough bearded men and their hardy little ponies, waiting by the sea's edge for the kegs of brandy, packets of lace and tobacco, or barrels of rum, which are shortly to be raced away up the rocky paths to the villages where the arrival of the "goods" is eagerly expected. This is well as far as it goes; but smuggling among the Cornishmen of old was not, as has been truly said, the outcome of a mere love of adventure or desire to cheat the revenue authorities.

Rather, it was something which was vital to the very existence of the people. The extreme poverty of the working classes, especially of those engaged in the precarious occupations of fishing and mining, created a condition which was peculiarly favourable to the development of this form of Free Trade. Without going so far as to say, as one writer has done, that the frequently recurring periods of economic stress *enforced* smuggling on the Cornish people, one can at least find in the state of the times some clue to the character of such a man as Captain Harry Carter, brother of the still more famous "King of Prussia," who, when already at the age of eighteen in command of a smuggling craft of his own, forbade all swearing and unseemly conversation on board his ship "under pain of punishment," and in later life when residing at Roscoff with a price upon his head, was in the habit of conducting religious services on Sunday afternoons for the benefit of the twenty or thirty other English smugglers staying in the town. "The men took off their hats," he notes in his diary after one of these occasions, "all very serious, no laffing, no trifling conversations." [1]

It is clear that such men regarded themselves not so much as smugglers as "fair traders," a term which they often applied to the enterprise in which they were engaged. They knew the law and, had it been in their power to do so, they would no doubt

[1] *Autobiography of a Cornish Smuggler*, 1749–1809. Edited by J. B. Cornish (1894).

have changed the law and legalized their position, but this being impossible, they set themselves above such a man-made institution. In doing so they clearly had the sympathy of more than one celebrated spokesman.

"It is impossible," declared Lord Holland in a speech before the House of Lords, 9 July, 1805, "totally to prevent smuggling, all that the legislature can do is to compromise with a crime which, whatever laws may be made to constitute it a high offence, the mind of man can never conceive as at all equalling in turpitude those acts which are breaches of clear moral virtues."

Adam Smith in his famous definition of a smuggler as "a person who, though no doubt highly blamable for violating the laws of his country, is frequently incapable of violating those of natural justice and who would have been in every respect an excellent citizen had not the laws of his country made that a crime which Nature never meant to be so," states the defence for smuggling with an even greater directness.[1]

On the other hand it must be admitted that there was a dark side to the smuggling trade, whose practitioners could not truthfully be described in all cases either as excellent citizens or as incapable, when provoked, of violating the laws of natural justice. Even so it must be remembered that if

[1] Cf., however, Dr. Johnson's definition of a smuggler as "A wretch who, in defiance of justice and the laws, imports or exports goods either contraband or without payment of the customs."

the smugglers were armed men, so in like manner were those whose business it was to prevent smuggling. If, under such circumstances, the conflicts which were bound to take place resulted in bloodshed and, occasionally, even loss of life, neither side could be held solely responsible. In most cases, however, it was the smugglers' reputation which suffered. Thus, when, in the year 1735, a quantity of rum which had been discovered in a barn near Fowey was being taken to the customhouse, we read that the excisemen were attacked by an armed body of smugglers who had acquired such a reputation for violence in that district that in the words of the official report: "If the officers attempt to make any seizure they go in danger of their lives, the smugglers having entered into a combination to rescue any person who shall be arrested."[1] How far the words "go in danger of their lives" should bear a literal interpretation it is difficult to say, seeing that the report, being an official one, must necessarily have been somewhat biased.

Nevertheless, there is plenty of evidence to show that serious clashes between the Government officers and the local population were at one time not infrequent. In 1768, William Odgers, one of the officers of the excise stationed at Porthleven, was murdered by a party of smugglers in a most barbarous manner. The case was made the subject of a searching inquiry and £100 reward was offered

[1] M. Oppenheim, *Victoria History of Cornwall*, 505.

by the commissioners to any one who would lay the necessary information. At the inquest, a verdict of wilful murder was returned against Melchisideck Kinsman, of Gwennap, and others unknown. The controller stated at the time that he feared four of the men implicated had escaped to Guernsey and Morlaix. Later, he advised the commissioners that he believed the men had not gone abroad but were skulking underground in the tin mines. The next year, he reported that £500 had been offered to Hampton, the principal witness for the Crown against the murderers, to go out of the country and stay away for two years. This, Hampton refused, and the commissioners granted him seven shillings a week, as he was afraid to go about on his ordinary work. In 1780, this man was receiving ten shillings a week. Eventually three of the supposed murderers gave themselves up and promised to effect the capture of Kinsman, which they succeeded in doing after an affray in which one of them was seriously wounded. All four were tried at the assizes, but, contrary to the opinion of the judge, and to the amazement of the whole court, were found not guilty. The collector stated in his report that there was no doubt that the jury had been bribed by Kinsman's relatives and that three of the jury had disappeared after the case.[1]

Another story, based though it is on tradition rather than on written evidence, will serve to

[1] Quoted by Mr. J. A. D. Bridger, *West Briton*, 22 October, 1931.

THE SMUGGLERS

illustrate further the violence to which the smuggling trade gave rise.

On a rough piece of moorland forming the western slope of Trencrom Hill, in the parish of Lelant, may still be seen two old granite-built cottages which locally go by the name of "Newcastle."[1] One of these, a century or more years ago, was occupied as a "kiddleywink" or beershop, a noted haunt of the smugglers who had excavated a cave (which may still be seen in the hedge outside) where supplies of contraband goods were regularly stored. At this particular time, the kiddleywink happened to be owned by two brothers, one of whom had joined the army. Finding, however, that the disciplined life of the service was less exhilarating than smuggling, the latter at length deserted and returned to his home where he lay for some time in hiding. It so happened that about this time the press-gang came into the district and getting wind of the deserter's whereabouts a party of soldiery suddenly descended one day upon the cottage. The door was opened by the other brother, who on learning the cause of the party's arrival, immediately put up a fight. The press-gang, however, proved too strong for him and in the course of the struggle he was killed. Meantime, the deserter brother, unaware of the desperate nature of the

---

[1] "Castle" is commonly used in a derisive sense in Cornwall, houses built in a pretentious style or in inconvenient situations being often nicknamed "Booby's Castle," a term corresponding to "—— Folly" in other shires.

fight proceeding below, had made a hole in the roof and succeeded in escaping to some hiding-place outside. On entering the house and finding the bird flown, the press-gang took their departure, and the deserter, though he long continued to live in the neighbourhood, was never troubled with their attentions again. The reason popularly given for this was that having killed one brother they were debarred from laying hands on the other, since the law did not allow of the taking of two men for one.[1]

It is certainly a fact that the excisemen were sometimes guilty of grave errors of judgment, as more than one innocent traveller learnt at the cost of his life. In the year 1799, a couple of preventive men, travelling between Bodmin and Truro, fell in with two persons whom, for some reason or other, they suspected of carrying smuggled goods. "This, however," as a correspondent states in the *Gentleman's Magazine*, 27 June, 1799, "not being the case, the suspects put up an obdurate resistance, until at length being overpowered by their desperate antagonists they were left dead on the spot. The excisemen then absconded." Whether the Government took any action in the matter does not appear. Perhaps, as in the case of the American judge of the pioneer days who, on finding that he had hanged an innocent man by mistake, is said to have "apologized" to the widow with the words: "Gee, marm, I guess you've got the laugh over

[1] Per Mr. R. J. Noall, of St. Ives.

us this time," the Government considered that they had already paid sufficiently in loss of prestige. Though this must have provided small consolation for the relatives of the unfortunate victims, there can be no doubt that keen satisfaction was felt by the countryside at large at such a discomfiture of the hated "sarchers." This, however, was not the only occasion on which the justice of the law miscarried with tragic results, as is revealed by the inscription on a tombstone, dated 1814, standing in the little churchyard of Mylor, near Falmouth:

> We have not a moment we can call our own.
> Officious zeal in luckless hour laid wait
> And wilful sent the murderous ball of Fate!
> James to his home, which late in health he left,
> Wounded returns—of life is soon bereft.

Notwithstanding the unconscious humour of the opening line, the memorial leaves little doubt of the strength of popular feeling which was aroused on this occasion. For in this case the victim of the excisemen's aggression was no mere stranger but a young man of the village who, returning in his boat one evening after having been out fishing, was fired upon by the officers and thus fatally wounded.

The smugglers themselves, however, sometimes made mistakes, and since attacks upon the detested minions of the law were generally made under cover of darkness, a hard fate occasionally awaited the individual who happened to look, ride or walk like an exciseman! One night in the early part of the last century, a Truro gentleman was riding home from Redruth at a late hour, when he suddenly found himself surrounded by a band of miners, who shouted: "Knack 'un down! Knack 'un down! and scat his head abroad 'pon the floor." The gentleman realizing the mistake which had been made quickly undeceived them, when the miners, in tones of deepest repentance, exclaimed: "Arreah! why 'tes Maister S—— from ovver to Trura, why we wud'n hurt a heer of hes head." Saying which they remounted Mr. S—— on his horse and escorted him far on his way home, finally taking leave with renewed apologies for the inconvenience which had been caused by his mistaken identity.

Though they hated the "sarchers" for their interference in what was locally regarded as an honest trade, the Cornish people could be generous even to their enemies when in distress. During one bitterly cold and pitch-black night in the month of December, 1805, two excise officers, travelling from Luxillian to Lostwithiel, lost their way, and after proceeding for several miles across country, at length found themselves in the desolate region of the Goss Moors. There they wandered for several hours, and at last became so exhausted that they sank down on the ground unable to proceed any farther. Fortunately for them, soon afterwards two tinners on their way to their night's labour chanced to hear their groans, and on discovering from whence they proceeded, immediately

THE SMUGGLERS

went to their relief, thereby in all probability saving them from death by exposure.[1]

In smuggling, indeed, as in other of the more adventurous games of life, the strands of humour and tragedy, generosity and meanness, were closely interwoven. Nowhere is this better illustrated than in the following story which was pieced together from traditional sources by that indefatigable researcher into "Old Cornwall"—Mr. R. J. Noall, of St. Ives.

During the earlier half of the last century, there flourished in west Cornwall a certain smuggler called Trevaskis, who had acquired more than a local reputation for his success in running "goods" upon the coast, and in finding safe hiding-places for them afterwards till the danger of discovery was past. It so happened that on one occasion a cargo was expected in a little cove to the west of St. Ives, a secluded spot admirably suited for the smuggler's needs. Among the few inhabitants of the valley was the owner of a grist mill, a simple old fellow who had never had any dealings with the smugglers himself, but who, on being approached by Trevaskis, good-naturedly gave permission for the storage of some of the goods on his property. This was done and all seemed well until a few weeks later when a party of excisemen arrived one day at the cove. The latter immediately began poking about the place, and in so doing discovered a nest of brandy-kegs cunningly concealed in one of the

[1] *Cornwall Gazette*, 21 December, 1805.

old man's furze ricks. The miller, needless to say, was terribly upset, dreading the loss of his reputation as an honest man even more than the legal consequences of his complicity. At length, however, he succeeded, in return for a bribe of £200, which comprised his life's savings, in getting the king's officer to hush the matter up. It would appear, however, that in the course of the inquiry the miller must have revealed the part which Trevaskis had had in the business, for shortly afterwards the "sarcher," hoping no doubt for another fat reward if he succeeded in catching so notorious a smuggler, called on the former and charged him with what he knew. The smuggler, being of a very different type from his confederate, told the exciseman bluntly that he "warn't going to pay no bribe," and that "they could put him up to Bodmin (the assize town) if they'd a mind to." To Bodmin, accordingly, he had to go, accompanied by the exciseman, who no doubt felt in high spirits. At Hayle, the couple boarded the train at the little station which may still be seen in Foundry Square, beneath the arches of the more modern railway line. Passing along under Clifton Terrace and through the grounds of the present Penmare House, the train at length reached the foot of "Steamer's Hill," near Angarrack, where a stationary engine at that time pulled the trucks up a steep incline to a point near the present Gwinear Road station. On this occasion, however, the train had not got more than half-way up the incline when the wire rope attached to the front carriage parted. Back rushed the trucks gathering terrible speed, till finally, reaching the bottom, they crashed into a bank and overturned. Strange to relate, few of the passengers were seriously hurt and only one was killed, that one being the exciseman! With no one who could now act as a witness against him, Trevaskis took his own release and returned home, amidst universal triumph, to his own village.

The story, however, ends on a tragic note. The miller's wife hearing of Trevaskis's escape never ceased to reproach her husband for his folly in having bribed the exciseman, and at length the worry of this so much preyed on the old man's mind that one morning he was found hanging dead from a beam in his own mill.

II

A complete history of Cornish smuggling has, for various reasons, never yet been attempted, and it is impossible, therefore, to assign any definite date to the beginning of the contraband trade. It is certain, however, that smuggling everywhere reached the zenith of its prosperity during the eighteenth century. In 1783, a committee which had been appointed by the Government to inquire into the matter, found that in some cases vessels of three hundred tons, manned by as many as a hundred men, were engaged in bringing "goods" across the Channel. "The most considerable of these vessels," states the Report, "are able to make seven or eight voyages a year. The largest of them can bring, in one freight, the enormous quantity of three thousand half-ankers of spirits, and ten or twelve tons of tea, whilst their strength is such as to enable them to bid defiance to the revenue cruisers. It is also a practice for the large armed vessels to take under convoy the small defenceless craft employed in the same trade. The landing of the cargo is regulated by signals, and the proceedings are guarded by scouts who give warning of any approach of strangers. The cargo is placed in wagons or on horses, being packed for that purpose in casks and oil-skin bags. Batteries

THE SMUGGLERS
(after Rowlandson)

(See page 18)

By kind permission of Mr. J. A. D. Bridger

THE SMUGGLERS

have been established on the coast to assist and protect these illicit landings. The commodities thus imported are distributed on the coast at little more than half the usual price, or brought to the metropolis under insurance, and delivered to retail traders or private housekeepers at about two-thirds of their proper price."[1]

Of this flourishing and important branch of the country's commerce Cornwall took its full share, and the records of the Cornish custom-houses of this date provide a complete corroboration of the truth of the above report. The hardihood and daring of the smugglers during this period knew no bounds. In 1748, the collector of customs at Penzance complained that a St. Keverne boat had anchored off the pier with contraband, and that the crew had sworn bitterly at the officers when they had approached, and endeavoured to knock out their brains with a boat-hook, besides throwing large stones at them, presumably from the ballast. On a subsequent occasion, a store of contraband wine was discovered at Gunwalloe. Finding no one who would lend them a "plough" (i.e. wheeled cart) for its removal, the officers sealed up the goods in a room. On calling two days later, however, with the required "plough" they discovered that the wine was gone. That evening, the collector and surveyor being in bed, four of the excisemen went off on their own, and found a quantity of goods in the charge of nine smugglers who

[1] Report of Committee on Smuggling, Parl. Pap. (1783).

c

threatened their lives with corn pikes. The excisemen came to an agreement that if they had the goods, the horses should go free. For this, however, they were severely reprimanded by their superior officers. Later on, the collector found at Ludgvan, on two different dates, thirty-three casks of brandy, forming part of this cargo. In June of the same year, he complained of the vast number and assurance of the smugglers. "They do smuggle so much," he writes, "that the seized brandy will not sell at the reserve price of 5s. 6d. a gallon, the smugglers supplying any quantity at 3s. 3d. a gallon."

In November, the collector reported that the custom warehouse had been broken open, the new locks shattered, and eighty-five gallons of brandy taken away. He added that but for an alarm which was raised by some, presumably, jealous neighbours, the whole store would have been cleared. A reward of ten pounds was offered but without result, whereupon the surveyor suggested that a free pardon and a more handsome reward should be offered to any one who would turn informer.

Later on in the same year, a warrant was obtained to arrest certain other smugglers. The constables, however, excused themselves from doing their duty on the grounds that the offenders had already fled, though it appears that the collector himself knew well enough that they might have been found had the men chosen to exert themselves.

In 1750, the collector seized a cargo of wool in a vessel lying off Penzance, but the justices (John Borlase, Christopher Hawkins, and Walter Borlase) dismissed the case, and the collectors were forced to ask for protection in case they should be served with writs by the smugglers, "who are got to that height they take all opportunity to insult the officers." On a subsequent occasion, a custom officer, whilst taking charge of a quantity of contraband found in a house at Marazion, had a silver spoon slipped into his pocket. This, he was charged by the smugglers with stealing. Happily for him the grand jury at the assizes threw out the bill. Some years later, two excisemen were severely injured by a certain James Rogers, of Breage, who attacked them with a hanger and a poleaxe whilst they were engaged in removing a cask of smuggled brandy from his house. For this, the officers were summoned by Rogers at Helston, on the charge of having entered upon his property without a warrant.

In 1774, the custom officers and a party of marines from the *Wolf* intercepted some smugglers, one of whom was shot dead by a marine. The coroner's jury found the latter guilty of murder. When the trial came on at Launceston, however, it was adjourned because no counsel would come to the town, the gaol fever being very bad there at the time.

In October 1751, a good haul of smugglers was made, including one Green, a notorious character.

The Penzance magistrates committed them to Launceston gaol, from which, however, they escaped in November "through the wall." On another occasion, the controller obtained evidence against a certain John Maddern, who struck a servant of the custom with a silver tankard and "cut his head in a vile manner, so that he was presently in a gore of blood." His informer, John Bodilley, afterwards came forward and said that when he swore the affidavit he was excessively overcome with liquor. Indeed, he went so far as to add that he had not been sober for several days.

In 1757, William Allen Cutler, of Penzance, broke open the custom warehouse and stole fifteen bags of tea, for which he was sentenced to seven years' transportation. The unfortunate officer, however, who was sent to retrieve the goods was promptly seized by two other smugglers, William Keigwin, of Mousehole, and John Yeoman (alias "Lean Jack"), and locked up in a room, from which he was not released until everything had been removed.

Smuggling in Mousehole, indeed, had arrived at such a pitch that the goods were commonly carried at noonday, the local exciseman excusing himself on one of these occasions by stating that he was confined to his bed through having been pelted with stones a few days before.

In 1759, the local controller entered a plea against seized goods being sold on the Scilly Islands, adding that there were "nought but smugglers there to sell the goods to." In 1761, he and his men seized a French cutter, having as its cargo one hundred and thirty-four half-ankers and twenty ankers (tubs) of brandy, four casks and two small bags of tea, and two bags of tobacco. This, the captain affirmed, was the entire lading of the vessel. Further search, however, revealed two other large casks of tea, cunningly hidden behind a false bulkhead. In this year, the collector again made representation that he should be allowed a boat in order to go out to vessels moored in the bay. "The inhabitants," he complained, "that have boats will never assist us, being in link with the smugglers."

Two years later, the new controller of Scilly asked that, as smuggling had got so bad, his men might be armed, and suggested that he might have sent him, six blunderbusses, six fusils, twenty pair of pistols of different sizes, twenty hangers, two dozen tucks, two dozen long tucks, and two dozen lanterns. Whether he was provided with these, does not appear.[1]

In any case, the arming of the excisemen in no way served to check the daring of the smugglers. In 1762, two hundred and eighteen ankers of brandy were landed by the men of "Proustock" (Port-houstock) in one night. Five years later, a smuggling fleet of nine sail of large boats and armed

[1] Penzance custom-house books, quoted by Mr. J. A. D. Bridger, *West Briton*, 22 October, 1931.

sloops passed out from Penzance, in full daylight, and under the very eyes of a man-of-war.

In 1771, a very fast-sailing sloop was boarded by the excise officers in Mounts Bay. She had a crew of twelve men, and was armed with eight carriage guns. The captain declared her cargo to be salt, but, on a search being made, a false bulkhead was discovered, behind which were artfully concealed some hundreds of dozens of silk handkerchiefs. In the ceiling of the cabin, which was hung with paper, were likewise found a large store of silk cambrics, muslin, lace, snuff-boxes, and trinkets.[1]

In 1772, a Penzance custom boat was plundered and sunk by a smuggler, and on 29 November of the same year, another sailed into Penzance harbour and carried off the revenue cutter *Brilliant*, which was lying there with captured cargo in her hold.[2] In 1775, two vessels lay off Penzance for three days discharging cargo, the custom collector looking on helplessly meanwhile, since every one ashore was either actively interested in the success of the "run," or a passive sympathizer. About the same time an excise ship off Padstow, instead of chasing, was chased into the port by a large Irish vessel which "by way of bravado fired seven guns at the mouth of the harbour and hung out a flag in triumph," afterwards sailing away to discharge

---

[1] Penzance custom-house books, quoted by Mr. J. A. D. Bridger, *West Briton*, 22 October, 1931.

[2] J. B. Cornish, *Cornish Magazine*, I, 118.

THE SMUGGLERS

her cargo at Newquay, in which place the smugglers and excise officers were stated to be on excellent terms. It was not uncommon, indeed, for a hundred horses to be awaiting the arrival of such cargoes here nearly every day of the week.[1]

Much of the reckless daring of the smugglers at this time was undoubtedly due to the fact that they enjoyed the protection of, and not infrequently an actual alliance with, persons of local standing and position. In 1770, the Mayor of Penzance was himself bound over in a considerable sum "not to be again guilty of smuggling." In 1779, four persons belonging to Poughill and Madron were prosecuted for having evaded the customs on smuggled goods to the extent of £18,600. They offered £160 in composition. One was a small farmer, whose property was worth but £15 a year; another a labourer, working for him. The two others were small yeomen. These men were, of course, financed by well-to-do people.

In 1780, the custom officials seized no less than 636 lb. of tea *in one day* in the parishes of Sithney and Breage. This valuable haul was derived almost entirely from the cottages, where the goods were concealed under beds or in haystacks. About the same time, a charge was brought against all the custom officials at Mousehole for themselves assisting the smugglers and receiving bribes.[2]

[1] M. Oppenheim, *Victoria History of Cornwall*.
[2] Penzance custom-house books, quoted by Mr. J. A. D. Bridger, *West Briton*, 22 October, 1931.

"The riches of the land and sea is in full gallop to France, and the countenance given to the smugglers by those whose business it is to restrain these pernicious practices hath brot 'm so bold and daring that nobody can venture to come near them with safety whilst they are at their work," wrote Mr. George Borlase in 1753. "The coasts here swarm with smugglers from the Land's End to the Lizard, so that I wonder the soldiers (which were late quartered here) should have been ordered off without being replaced by others."[1] One would have thought that Mr. Borlase, being a Cornishman, and knowing something of the propensities of the local squires (who were also the magistrates), might have found a possible answer to his own question. Be that as it may, it is quite clear from the scale on which much of the smuggling of these days was conducted that a large amount of capital was invested in the trade. The vessels used in the Cornish ports ranged, as we know, from fifty to two hundred and fifty tons burthen, and were often heavily armed. Mevagissey-built craft in particular were so noted for their fast-sailing qualities as to be in demand from Dover to the Land's End. Some of these luggers carried a thousand yards of canvas in their mainsail, and with a fair wind would cross the Channel in eight hours. "In those days," wrote Mr. Matthias Dunn, "the purchase price of a cargo of brandy for one of these

[1] Lanisley Letters, printed in *Journal* of Royal Institution of Cornwall (1881), XXIII, 374-9.

ships in France or the Channel Islands was £1,500, and the same would be sold for £3,000 in this country. As a consequence, when smuggling was in its full swing, money became so plentiful that neighbours lent guineas to each other by the handful, not stopping to count, or being so particular as to reckon by ones or twos."[1]

As the result of the encouragement and protection which they received on land, and the absence of interference at sea, owing to the forces of the navy being otherwise requisitioned during the European wars, the latter half of the eighteenth century was indeed the Golden Age of smuggling. "In the western part of this county," wrote Mr. Edward Giddy, of Tredrea, to the chief custom officer in 1778, "smuggling, since the soldiers have been drawn off, has been carried on almost without control. Irish wherries, carrying fourteen, sixteen, or more guns, and well manned, frequently land large quantities of goods in defiance of the officers of the customs and excise, and their crews, armed with swords and pistols, escort the smugglers a considerable distance from the sea. In this way, goods are carried from one part of the country to another almost every night. About a fortnight since, a large wherry landed, according to the best information I can obtain, from fifteen hundred to two thousand ankers of spirits (containing $9\frac{1}{2}$ gallons on an average), about twenty tons of tea, and other kinds of smuggled goods, on a sandy beach in

[1] *Western Morning News*, 8 March, 1930.

Mounts Bay, between the towns of Penzance and Marazion. This beach lies near a public road which, whilst the goods were discharging, was filled with armed men, in order to stop every traveller in whom they could not confide, till the goods were safely lodged in the country.

"A few days after, two officers got information that a very considerable quantity of goods was concealed in the house and premises of a well-known smuggler. They obtained from me a search warrant, but were forcibly hindered from executing it by four men, one armed with a pistol and a large whip, the others with sticks and bludgeons. They were told that if they persisted they would have their brains blown out. As the law now stands, I fear a criminal prosecution would have been useless for the reason, which it shocks me to mention, that a Cornish jury would certainly acquit the smugglers.

"These, my lord, are facts. It would be mere pedantry to attempt to describe to your lordship the shocking effects, the moral and political consequences of smuggling carried to such a daring height, but I cannot help saying that perjury, drunkenness, idleness, poverty, and contempt of the law, and a universal corruption of manners are, in this neighbourhood, too plainly seen to accompany it.

"It is a very unlucky circumstance that Patrick Plunkett, who was lately discharged from our county gaol by an order from your lordship, should have escaped without a prosecution, for he is a very daring fellow, and I fear his advice, example, and impunity will increase the audacity and inhumanity of the smugglers which the civil power, such at least as we can obtain from it, seems too weak to oppose with effect.—Yours etc., Edward Giddy." [1]

The state of affairs which the writer describes was by no means confined to west Cornwall, but appears to have been more or less general to the county at this period. "I well remember, some time before the conclusion of the peace," stated a writer from St. Columb in 1765, "that having occasion to land some goods out of one of my vessels at the port of Padstow, my servants set out some time before day, but by fine moonlight, when, crossing the common about three miles from us, they met sixty horses having each three bags of tea on them of fifty-six or fifty-eight pounds weight. All this was landed on a beach about two miles to the west of Padstow, and carried from thence through this county and into Devon." [2]

Though the contemporary records are soberly worded, they suffice to show the influence which the astonishing exploits of the smuggler kings of this date must have had upon the public imagination. Nor is it strange that in course of time and

[1] Penzance custom-house books, quoted in *West Briton*, 22 October, 1931.
[2] Letters from William Rawlings to Earl of Dartmouth.—Hist. MSS. Comm., XV, 176.

through oft recounting, the lives and actions of such men should at length have passed beyond history and become enshrined in popular romance.

Of all the figures associated by tradition with the smuggling trade of the north coast of Cornwall during the eighteenth century, none has acquired a more lasting notoriety than that of "Cruel Coppinger," the Dane, concerning whom the Rev. R. S. Hawker has catalogued a series of dreadful tales in his book, entitled *Footprints of Former Men in Far Cornwall*. Very little is actually known of this wild and, perhaps, half-mythical personage. Local tradition, however, relates that one day in the midst of a fearful storm a foreign-rigged vessel was seen in the offing, drifting in towards the shore. Whether or not she was actually wrecked was never known, for the ship was soon afterwards lost sight of in the driving clouds and rain. One man, however, came ashore from her, swimming powerfully through the boiling surf. Wrapped in a cloak that he is said to have torn from the shoulders of an old woman who was on the beach, the stranger leaped up behind a farmer's daughter who had ridden down to see the wreck, and was taken by her to her father's house, where he was fed, clothed, and most hospitably received. He was a fine, handsome, well-built man, and gave himself out as being highly connected in his own country. He soon won the young woman's affections, and at her father's death, which occurred not long after, he easily induced her to marry him. The union was not a happy one, and, fortunately perhaps, there was only one child—a deaf and dumb idiot who inherited his father's cruel disposition and delighted in torturing all living things. It is even said that he cunningly killed one of his young playmates. After his marriage, Coppinger made himself captain of an organized band of smugglers, and through his black deeds quickly earned the title by which he is remembered. Hawker in his book refers to Coppinger's ship as the *Black Prince*, and says that he had it built for himself in Denmark, and that men who had made themselves in any way obnoxious to him on land were carried on board this vessel, and compelled, by fearful oaths, to enrol themselves as members of her crew. Although Hawker was a novelist, rather than an historian, there is no reason for doubting this particular assertion. In the year 1835, an old man of the age of ninety-seven, told Miss M. A. Courtney, of Penzance, that when a youth he had been abducted in a precisely similar manner, and had only been ransomed by his friends after two years' service on board a smuggling craft. "And all," said the old man, very simply, "because I happened to see one man kill another, and they thought I should mention it."

Hawker, who delighted in flights of the imagination, whether his own or those of the simple country-folk among whom he lived, credits Coppinger with a wondrous and fearful end. His account, however, tallies so closely with that given by Bottrell of the passing of a wicked and notorious wrecker near St. Just that we prefer quoting from the latter on account of its admirable word-painting. "At length," states this writer, "the time came for the fiend to claim his own. Several parsons and other pious folks were sent for and readily came, for the dying sinner was rich. Although it was harvest-time and high-by-day, the old wrecker's chamber became, at times, as dark as night. The parsons saw the devil in the room when others could not; and by their reading they drove him to take many shapes, but for all that he would not be put out, and at last, when he took the form of a fly and buzzed about the dying wretch, they saw that it was vain for them to try any longer. During all the time the exorcists were thus engaged the chamber seemed—by the sound—to be filled with the sea splashing around the bed, and waves were heard as if surging and breaking against the house, though it was a good bit inland. Whilst this was taking place at the dying man's bedside, two men, who were about harvest work in one of his fields near the cliff, heard a hollow voice, as if coming from the sea, which said, 'The hour is come but the man is not come.' Looking in the direction from whence the words proceeded, they saw no person, but far out to sea they beheld a black, heavy, square-rigged ship, with all sail set, coming in fast, against wind and tide and not a hand to be seen aboard her. She came so close under the

THE SMUGGLERS

cliff that only her topmast could be seen; when black clouds—that seemed to rise out of the deep—gathered around her, and extended thence straight to the dying man's chamber. The harvesters, terrified at the sight of this ship-of-doom so near them, ran up to the town-place, just at the moment as the old sinner died, when his dwelling shook as if about to fall. Everybody, in great fright, rushed out and saw the black clouds roll off towards the death-ship, which at once sailed away—amidst a blaze of lightning—over the sea, and disappeared. The weather immediately cleared, and nothing unusual occurred until a few men assembled to put the wrecker's ghastly remains quickly off the face of the earth. Then, as the coffin was borne towards the churchyard, the sky again became suddenly overcast, and a tempest sprang up with such violence that they could scarcely keep on their legs to reach the churchyard stile, where such sheets of blinding lightning flashed around them that they dropped the coffin and rushed into the church. The storm having at length abated, they ventured out to find nothing of the coffin but its handles and a few nails, all else having been set on fire and consumed by the lightning." [1]

So in like manner was Cruel Coppinger overtaken by his fate, as the story was related by the old droll-tellers from whom Hawker derived his account. Despite the mythical nature of this and many of

[1] William Bottrell, *Traditions and Hearthside Stories of West Cornwall*, second series, 247–9.

the other stories which are associated with him, there is reason for supposing that an actual smuggler of this name did at one time flourish on the north coast of Cornwall. It would appear also that he amassed enough money by his ill-doings to purchase a small freehold estate near the sea, the title-deeds of which, bearing his signature, were in existence not long since.[1]

[1] M. A. Courtney, *Cornish Feasts and Folklore*, 91.

Gibson, Penzance

III

It has often been claimed that the teaching of Wesley and the spread of the Methodist movement was responsible for putting an almost complete check upon smuggling. In point of fact, however, this was far from being the case, since, as already shown, smuggling and Methodism long went hand in hand, and impossible as the association may seem to-day it is none the less true, that in the past some of the most notorious of Cornish smugglers were also staunch supporters of the dissenting cause. Even their natural enemies, the officers of the excise, were fain to admit the sterling qualities of many of these men, the collector of custom at Penzance in 1771 describing Richard Pentreath of Mousehole, otherwise "Doga," as "an honest man in all his dealings though a notorious smuggler," whilst Thomas Mann, of the same place, is likewise spoken of in the official records as a "reputed smuggler," but "an honest man."[1]

In all the annals of Cornish smuggling, no better illustration is provided of this strange, but not entirely incomprehensible, mixture of honest bravery with an inclination to break a certain man-made law, than in the case of the Carter family of Prussia Cove.

[1] J. B. Cornish, *Cornish Magazine*, I, 118.

The most famous member of this gang, John Carter, the "King of Prussia," is still remembered on account of the high standard of integrity which he adopted in all his commercial dealings. Characteristic of this is the time-honoured story which relates how, on a certain occasion, he broke open the custom-house store at Penzance in order to recover some goods which had been confiscated during his absence from home, explaining to his comrades who demurred at the risk, that he had agreed to deliver the same to his customers by a specified date, and that to fail in this obligation would be to forfeit his reputation as an honest trader. Nor is it yet forgotten how, when the excisemen arrived the next morning and found that the place had been broken open, they said amongst themselves, "John Carter has been here, and we know it because he is an upright man, and has taken away nothing which was not his own."[1]

Such, indeed, were the ethics of Cornish smuggling in its palmiest days and among its most celebrated practitioners. It is not so surprising, therefore, in the light of this, to find that the diary of Harry Carter,[2] brother of "the king," reads more like a circuit minister's commonplace book than the annals of a daring smuggler, and whilst page after page is filled with religious "experiences," only such occasional entries as "bought a cutter of

[1] J. B. Cornish, *Cornish Magazine*, I, 118.
[2] *The Autobiography of a Cornish Smuggler*, edited by J. B. Cornish (1894).

160 tons and 19 guns," or "surprised by two man-of-war boats while landing at Costan," show that the worthy captain was still engaged in a worldly vocation of a strangely different nature.

The story of Prussia Cove, and of the daring adventurers whose deeds have made it famous for all time, has been well told by the late Mr. J. B. Cornish, of Penzance, in an interesting article contributed to the *Cornish Magazine*. The very name of the cove (which lies immediately to the eastward of Cuddan Point in Mounts Bay) is John Carter's own, it being said that the latter, when a boy and playing at soldiers with other children, so regularly claimed to be the "King of Prussia," that for his sake the cove where he dwelt at length lost its older name of Porthleah and became known as "The King of Prussia's Cove." The degree of fame which attended the doings of the local "king" during the hey-day of his prosperity is amusingly illustrated by the story told of a sailor who on his return between voyages during the Napoleonic wars used regularly to visit an old farmer residing in the neighbourhood of Gwithian.

"Well, what's the news this time, my son?" was the question which greeted the traveller on one of these occasions.

"Why, the latest thing I've heard, Uncle Caleb, is that the King of Prussia has suffered a big loss."

"My dear life, that so, es 'a?" exclaimed the farmer. "I tell 'ee, Maister Joe, I'm downright sorry for that man. 'Twas only last month he lost nigh upon forty ankers of brandy—by information, so I 'm told!"[1]

There is little doubt that for the majority of poor people living in west Cornwall at this time, there was only *one* King of Prussia, a fact which is the less marvellous when one recollects that newspapers were still a rarity in all but the houses of the well-to-do, whilst the deeds of the smuggling king at their doors had reached a pitch of notoriety almost eclipsing the fame of Bonaparte himself.

The site chosen by the Carter family for the headquarters of their operations had every natural advantage to recommend it. "A spot," as Mr. J. B. Cornish has said, "so sheltered and secluded that it is impossible to see what boats are in the little harbour until one literally leans over the edge of the cliff above; a harbour cut out of the solid rock and a roadway with wheel-tracks, partly cut and partly worn, climbing up the face of the cliff on either side of the cove, caves and remains of caves everywhere, some of them with their mouths built up which are reputed to be connected with the house above by secret passages—these are still existing trademarks left by one of the most enterprising smuggling gangs that Cornwall has ever known." In this favoured spot lived and reigned John Carter, the King of Prussia, during the years 1770 to 1807. Many a stirring and exciting tale has been recorded by Mr. Cornish of the exploits of that adventurous reign, probably the best known

[1] Per Miss B. Vivian.

being that of the smugglers firing upon a revenue cutter from their little battery which lay stationed on the point between Bessie's and the "King's" Cove.[1] This act, though it marks an epoch in the history of Cornish smuggling, was in reality purely one of bravado, little damage being done, either by the guns of the smugglers or by the return fire which was opened upon the latter from the decks of the ship-of-war.

Indeed, the annals of Mounts Bay smuggling as a whole are remarkably free from tales of bloodshed. How far this was due to restraint on the part of the smugglers, or to the tact of the revenue men in keeping out of harm's way, it is, of course, not easy to say. For it is clear that very often when the excise officers were not actually terrorized, "they wore fog spectacles with bank-note shades," as a writer has said. Smuggling, indeed, was carried on even in the official Falmouth packet boats, running to and from Lisbon and the West Indies, and wine from the former was sold in Cornwall at this time at little more than half the ordinary price. "The captains themselves," states a contemporary, "smuggle large quantities, and connive at the men doing the same, not allowing them sufficient wages whereon to live without it. When the *Vansittart*, East Indiaman, recently arrived in Falmouth, people came together on horse and foot from twenty miles around and flocked on board every day, including Sundays, as to a fair.

[1] "Annals of the Smugglers," *Cornish Magazine*, I, 122.

Muslins, silks, and other valuable and dutiable goods were sold to the value of at least £5,000." [1]

It was a notorious fact that scarcely any seizures were ever made at this port by the excise.

With a whole countryside in league against them, it is small wonder that the excisemen occasionally showed themselves not over-zealous in the cause of duty, preferring to take the line of least resistance rather than risk their lives in the attempt of an impossible task. Chief among the aiders and abettors of the smugglers on land were the miners and alluvial tin streamers, and liquor brought ashore anywhere in the neighbourhood of Penzance was always certain of a safe hiding-place among the stream-banks and moors in the secluded valleys of the West Penwith mining area. Many of the streamers themselves, moreover, indulged in smuggling, and during the summer-time, when water was scarce, found a profitable outlet for their activities in the taking of three or four trips to Roscoff, in Brittany, for the purchase of brandy, silk handkerchiefs, lace and other articles of contraband. "Our Free Traders ran but little risk then," writes Mr. Bottrell, "as there was no Preventive Service of any note. If the revenue cutters came near our western land their crews dreaded more to fall in with the Cornish traders than our smugglers ever feared the king's men. As for the riding officers and excisemen, they would rather ride anywhere than on the cliffs in the dark

[1] M. Oppenheim, *Victoria History of Cornwall*, 506.

nights when the beacon fires blazed from the rocky cairns to guide the smugglers' boats into the coves. Still less would the officers care to venture among the stream-leats and bogs where scores of ankers (barrels) of brandy used formerly to be left, till the innkeepers, gentry, and other regular customers wanted them. Now and then, of course, there was a bit of a shindy between the streamers and excisemen for mere sham, and in return the smugglers would leave an anker or two to be taken, in places where they never kept their stock. This served for a decoy, and the Government crew knew well enow that that was their share, and they had better not look for any more." [1]

During those good old roystering days, many of the young "West Country" blades, sons of the yeoman squires who farmed the ancestral tenements of West Penwith, were in the habit of fitting out fast-sailing, well-armed little craft which they kept in Porth-gwarra, Porth-Curnow, and other of the secluded coves which lie deep-hidden in that romantic strip of coastline between Penzance and the Land's End. The work of seed-time or harvest being over, the boats would be got ready for a trip to France, and they and their crews would then disappear for weeks or months on end, often returning at the end of that time with goods of such richness and rarity as an over-curious person would scarcely have credited as being *bought* from our neighbours across the

[1] *Traditions and Hearthside Stories of West Cornwall* (1870), 70.

Channel. Little inquiry was made, however, of the exact doings of these wild young rovers when away on their mysterious voyages, and if rumours occasionally hinted at some rich foreign merchantman having been relieved of portions of its cargo, they were soon quieted; for at that time little distinction was made between smuggler, privateer, and pirate. Indeed, with money to spend on one and all, with their gifts of jewels and lace for the women, and their brandy, rum, and tobacco for the squire, such reckless young adventurers were the heroes of the hour, and for long after their return the halls of the old decaying mansions which were their homes resounded far into the night with the shouts and songs of the feasters, who kept open house for all who cared to join them in their wild and care-free revels.[1]

[1] *Traditions and Hearthside Stories of West Cornwall* (1870), 192 et seq.

IV

Whilst the wars with France continued, cutters and luggers armed with eighteen or twenty guns apiece, and manned by reckless adventurers of this sort, had more or less their own way in the Channel between Ushant and the Smalls. With the declaration of the Peace of Amiens, however, in 1802, the armed smuggler began to prove a definite source of embarrassment to the Government, and measures were put in hand to stay their practices, which were rightly considered a menace to our international relationships. This decision, however, was regarded in Cornwall with a lack of enthusiasm which would appear to signify that considerable interests were at stake. "A squadron of frigates being ordered to cruise on the Cornish coasts against the smugglers," comments the *Cornwall Gazette*, a Tory newspaper, on 13th February, 1802, "has raised a formidable idea in the public mind of the extent of the illicit trade carried on here. We shall be much surprised, however, if these frigates shall, at the end of twelve months, have seized as much spirits as will be equal to the regular consumption of their crews. The fact is that while the war establishment is kept up, some employment must be found for it—'When children are doing nothing they are doing mischief.'"

Despite such protestations, however, the surveillance of the Government forces at this time, on sea and land, was not without its effect. Whether through the over-recklessness of their crews or because their malpractices had marked them out for special attention, Polperro boats seem to have suffered most during these years. Among the losses sustained by this port may be mentioned the *Unity*, which after having made, as it is said, no less than five hundred successful trips across the Channel, was at length captured with one hundred and seventy casks of spirits on board, besides large quantities of tobacco. As a measure of the smugglers' daring, it is interesting to note that when seized this vessel was lying in Plymouth Sound, with the king's ships ranked about her on every side! The *Expedition* of Polperro met with a like fate during the same month, when she was brought into Plymouth with nine hundred ankers of brandy in her hold, "besides bale goods and tobacco." About six weeks later, another of the Polperro fleet, the *Three Friends*, fell to the king, being surprised by H.M.S. *Spitfire* whilst discharging her illicit cargo into boats outside her home port. On this occasion, as in that of the *Lottery*, another Polperro capture, we find the crew making armed resistance, and one smuggler was killed on the spot. A few months later, yet another Polperro craft, the lugger *Providence*, was seized by a revenue cutter when on her voyage home from Guernsey with eight hundred ankers on board.[1]

[1] C. K. C. Andrew, *Western Morning News*, 13 March, 1930.

THE SMUGGLERS 43

Polperro, however, was not the only sufferer. In February 1802, the *Nymphe* frigate captured, and sent into Plymouth, a smuggling cutter of Fowey with nine hundred and forty-four ankers of spirits and some dry goods on board,[1] whilst in the following month we read of one hundred and thirty kegs of spirits being seized in the parish of St. Hilary by the officers of the excise.[2]

Such incidents, though they read coldly enough upon paper, were often of an exciting nature, and took place under romantic circumstances. On one occasion in the summer of 1801, a smuggler, with two ankers of brandy on the horse under him, was discovered by an exciseman on the steep and precipitous road leading down to King Harry Passage on the River Fal. Without waiting to be challenged, the smuggler immediately rode off at full speed, closely pursued by the officer who was also on horseback. Despite the breakneck speed with which he descended the hill, the smuggler, on reaching the passage, found his pursuer pressing so hard upon him that he immediately plunged his horse into the water, in an attempt to gain the opposite shore. The horse, however, had not swum halfway over, before, exhausted with fatigue and the load on his back, he was on the point of sinking. Realizing this, the intrepid rider slid from the animal's back, and with his knife cut the slings which bound the ankers. Swimming then alongside

[1] *Cornwall Gazette*, 6 February, 1802.
[2] *Cornwall Gazette*, 13 March, 1802.

his horse, the smuggler exerted himself in the attempt to keep the animal's head above water, but all to no purpose, for the horse was drowned, and the man only with the utmost difficulty reached the opposite shore. Meantime, the less mettlesome exciseman had halted on the nearer bank, from whence he surveyed the ineffectual struggle; afterwards, with the help of the ferryman, getting possession of the kegs.[1]

Still, as events proved, the anxiety of Cornwall at the possibility of any serious check to smuggling at this time was premature. With renewal of hostilities in 1803, the forces of the Crown were once again diverted to more pressing matters, and smuggling took on a new lease of life. One might even say that the Government was in some measure responsible for stimulating it. For in the early months of the war, owing to the need of men for the services and home defence, Royal Proclamation was made that any smuggler who had fled the country should, provided he was not charged with murder, be permitted to return without fear of arrest, on his entering into bond to refrain from smuggling practices for the future. Copies of this proclamation were posted in all Cornish villages, and it was not long before the news filtered through to those who were lying in exile overseas. Among the first to take advantage of the amnesty was a certain Christopher Pollard, of Madron. The latter had been charged some years before with

[1] *Cornwall Gazette*, 29 August, 1801.

obstructing and assaulting the revenue officers, and had fled to Guernsey in order to escape the consequences of his crimes. He now returned to Cornwall and signed the requisite bond, his brother, Joseph Pollard, standing surety for the sum of £200. But for him, as for many another, the allurements of the old adventurous life were too strong, and little more than six months had elapsed before Pollard, as appears from a brief to counsel, dated 1805, was again concerned in a charge of smuggling. The prosecution states that on this occasion the accused had assaulted the officers of H.M. excise when occupied in their duty at Sennen, and had incited a crowd of three or four hundred persons to attack the excisemen with a view to carrying off the smuggled goods which they had captured and were defending on the beach. This landing was indeed a valuable one, consisting as it did of one thousand gallons of brandy, one thousand gallons of rum, one thousand gallons of Geneva, and five hundred pounds of tobacco. In addition to the general charge of inciting the mob, Pollard was accused of having offered £100 for the rescue of a hundred ankers of the spirits and "*of using other violent and improper language.*" The counsel for the defence admitted that Pollard was part-owner of these goods, but stated that what had actually happened was that on going to Sennen he had found the cargo in the possession of the revenue authorities, and that so far from inciting the mob to a rescue he had gone straight home, only calling in on the excise officer at Newlyn in order to advise him to go to Sennen at once "lest any unforeseen circumstances might ensue." It further appears that in the evening of the same day on which the cargo had been landed, Pollard was in a public-house at Penzance trying to sell a yoke of oxen to a farmer of Nancothnan, named Pool. The latter afterwards accompanied Pollard to Sennen and agreed to provide him with horses wherewith to remove the cargo in return for the promise of a cask of brandy for his own use—"he having a number of workmen and tradesmen about him at the time." On arriving at the beach, however, about eleven o'clock at night and finding a huge crowd firing muskets and throwing stones at the excisemen, "they decided that that was no place for them to stay for that they would be killed." So both returned home.

The principal witness for the prosecution was a certain Anne George. This woman, it appears, was a person of notorious character. At the time of the trial she is described as being the wife of Joseph George who, up to a short time before, had been the keeper of the Sennen inn—a place which had the reputation of being "the resort of all the idle blackguards in the county." During the time in which he had kept the inn, Joseph George had acted as a smuggling agent for his landlord, a well-to-do farmer of the parish, named Dionysius Williams. Presuming on the secret hold which

THE SMUGGLERS 47

they possessed over their landlord, through the knowledge of his illicit transactions, the Georges had for some time refused to pay any rent for the inn, and at length the owner, very unwisely, had decided to eject them. Infuriated by this, the innkeeper's wife had thereupon turned king's evidence against Williams, and reaped her revenge in seeing the latter served with a long term of imprisonment.

The villainy of the woman's character, however, is best revealed by the account, given in the same brief, of a quarrel which she had had some years previously with her brother-in-law, John George, over a few pounds of tobacco. In this case also she had turned king's evidence, accused the victim of her malice of firing on a revenue officer, and so incriminated him that the poor wretch was actually convicted and hanged on 5th June, 1802. In a district in which almost every inhabitant had probably had some hand in smuggling at one time or another, the presence of such a malicious and wholly unscrupulous informer caused widespread fear, and no doubt accounted for the difficulty which was experienced in obtaining witnesses for the defence. "The terror and dismay, indeed, which this woman has been the means of spreading throughout the county are not to be described," stated the counsel's brief. "Independent of the present prosecution no less than five persons have been capitally indicted by her means, one of whom has already been executed, and so callous is her conscience, and deadly her revenge, that persons who may have given her slight cause for offence are now trembling for fear of the consequences, expecting to be made the next victim of the detestable passion with which she is actuated." [1]

It was probably due to the discreditable character of the chief witness against him, rather than to any proof of his own innocence, that Pollard in this case owed his acquittal. His narrow escape from justice, however, appears to have taught him no lesson, and ten years later he was serving a term of imprisonment in Devon gaol as the result of his having been arrested off Plymouth when in the possession of a large quantity of smuggled goods.

It was not until the actual signing of peace after Waterloo that the changes which mark a definite epoch in the history of smuggling came about. The termination of the war, whilst it greatly augmented the ranks of the smugglers through the release of men from the services, also had the effect of enabling the Government at long last to deal seriously with the contraband trade. In 1816–17 a new and much more efficient preventive force was established along the south coast of England, and a regular watch began to be kept upon the activities of the smaller fishing coves and ports. The consequences seem to have borne particularly hardly upon the inhabitants of the Scilly Islands, who had hitherto looked upon smuggling as their chief

[1] Brief to Counsel, seen by kind permission of Mr. J. A. D. Bridger, Penzance.

THE SMUGGLERS

source of revenue. In 1818, seven magistrates from Penzance and the district went over to the Scillies to make a report on the condition of the people. They concluded their findings with the following interesting statement: "And above all, by the entire suppression of smuggling on these islands (a measure which has been accomplished by the preventive boat system established there) the islanders, who had too long and too successfully depended on their contraband trade, are now deprived of their chief means of support."[1]

Actually, the claim that smuggling had been entirely suppressed on the Scillies at this date was somewhat too sweeping, for records show that the trade continued to linger in the islands for many years after this. Here, as elsewhere, however, the increasing watchfulness of the preventive service was giving the smugglers serious cause for concern. About this time, therefore, the latter began to change their methods and, abandoning the large, heavily-armed craft which they had hitherto employed, took to a smaller class of vessel. For this, the half-decked fishing boats of Cawsand Bay and other ports along the south coast proved particularly suited. During the ten years 1832-42 no less than fifty-two boats and eighty-one men belonging to Cawsand were engaged in the smuggling trade with the ports across the Channel—a fairly good record for one village.[2]

[1] *West Briton*, 22 October, 1931.
[2] H. N. Shore, *Smuggling Days and Smuggling Ways*, 109 (edn. 1929).

Roscoff was now the chief entrepôt of the smugglers, as Guernsey had been in earlier times. In one month, November 1824, the following Cornish smuggling craft left Roscoff: *Marie I* of Cawsand, with cargo for the west of Dodman; *Marie II*, of Cawsand, for Hemwick Cove; *Cruzier*, of Polperro, for St. Austell Bay; *Ant*, of Mevagissey, for the Black Head; *Arethusa*, of Cawsand, for St. Austell Bay; and *Exchange*, of Polperro, for near the Black Head.[1]

In March 1832, a "well-informed" correspondent reported from Roscoff that "smuggling had not been carried on so extensively at any time during the last twenty years as it is now." In the following year, the same writer gave information concerning nineteen west-country boats which had arrived or departed from this port within a fortnight.[2] These were, for the most part, small craft, varying from nine to a hundred tons. Crossing the hundred miles of water between Roscoff and the Cornish coast in the bitter gales of a hard winter can have been no child's play even in decked vessels of this size, and, as Commander Shore has written, one can scarcely imagine what it must have been in the open boats, to which the more adventurous souls entrusted their persons and their cargoes.[3] Nevertheless, there were always men to be found who were eager to play the risky game,

[1] H. N. Shore, *Smuggling Days*, 99.
[2] H. N. Shore, *Smuggling Days*, 102, 105.
[3] H. N. Shore, *Smuggling Days* 110 (edn. 1929).

and willing to stake their all in the attempt to bring in the articles of contraband for which there was still such a ready sale.

A story told of Prussia Cove somewhat after the days of the "king," serves to illustrate the humours of smuggling as also the hardiness and endurance of the men who were engaged at this period in the trade. On a certain occasion, two Prussia Cove men were returning home from Roscoff in a small sailing boat well laden with contraband. The wind having dropped, they had been forced for the latter part of their crossing to labour at the oars and, thinking to save themselves the last few miles, decided to put in to Mullion. On arriving here, however, they found two excisemen waiting on the beach. Exhausted after their long and arduous passage, the smugglers offered five pounds in order to be allowed to land. Bribery in this case, however, proved of no avail, and so with heavy hearts they bent themselves once more to the task of rowing on to the Cove. Meantime, the officers mounted their horses and kept pace with them along the cliffs. Just short of the Cove, the smugglers passed out of sight of the excisemen behind a headland, and here, much to their delight, they found a Cover out in his boat, hauling crab-pots. Making good use of their opportunity, they quickly exchanged the contents of their boat with that of their neighbour, and rowed on their way. They had hardly drawn into the Cove before the officers arrived, and immediately set about a search—but in vain! It was not until some hours later, when the coast was once more clear, that an innocent-looking fisherman came into shore bringing with him a catch which is not often taken in crab-pots.[1]

In 1818, there arose a curious case which illustrates not only the ingenuity of the smugglers, but the shady practices to which the legal fraternity were willing to lend themselves in the cause of such clients. About this time, two St. Just smugglers, named Oats and Permewan, had been very successful in running goods upon the north coast of Cornwall. Their activities extended over a considerable area, and in the course of a few months they are stated to have landed no less than six cargoes. In order to ensure greater secrecy, the smugglers had adopted the method of employing an agent — by name Pridham — to whom they made payment for the goods and whose duty it was to settle their accounts with the French merchants. For some time the arrangement appears to have worked fairly well. At length, however, a report reached the smugglers that the remittances, which were always promptly made on their part, were not being forwarded by their agent. Realizing that the latter was no longer to be trusted, the smugglers decided to sever the connection. On this, Pridham announced that he would turn king's evidence against them. A meeting between Permewan and the agent was accordingly arranged,

[1] J. B. Cornish, *Cornish Magazine*, I, 123.

with a view, if possible, to buying off the evidence, although the lawyer in charge of the smugglers' defence must have realized as clearly as his clients that there was but slight hope of achieving this. It appears, however, that a short time before the meeting was to take place, Permewan suggested that he had doubts as to Pridham's ability to recognize him, seeing that they had only met on two occasions, for a few minutes at a time. They therefore decided to take the risk of dressing up a brother of Permewan's in the latter's clothes, and sending him to Devonshire to the appointed interview. In the meantime, the smuggler brother was at pains on the day on which the meeting took place to be seen walking about the streets of Penzance, where he was spoken to by all and sundry. By this means an indisputable alibi was established, which so entirely discredited Pridham's evidence as to render it wholly worthless in a court of law.[1]

By the forties of the last century, the palmiest days of Cornish smuggling were over. Nevertheless, the trade continued on a fairly extensive scale; whilst the smugglers themselves had lost none of their former daring. On 18 September, 1840, we learn that H.M. custom-house at Helford, within the port of Gweek, was attacked by a body of men, "consisting, as it is supposed, of upwards of thirty persons, who broke open the heavy doors and strong locks, and robbed the cellars of one hundred and twenty-six kegs of contraband brandy

[1] Brief to Counsel, seen by permission of Mr. J. A. D. Bridger.

(each keg containing four and a half gallons of spirit) which had been seized some days before at Coverack." The burglars commenced their work about 1 a.m. and in the course of half an hour had succeeded in removing all the kegs except three, which they left for the benefit of the officers at Helford! The man and his wife who lived at the custom-house had heard the sound of the cellar doors being broken open, but had been afraid to give the alarm, which, indeed, they could not well have done in any case, as the house was a remote building nearly three-quarters of a mile from any other dwelling. From the tracks of the wheels which were seen next day, it was supposed that at least three wagons had been employed in removing the spirit, a fact which accounted for the rapidity with which the whole business had been effected.[1]

The smugglers, however, were no longer in the position of being able to "get away with it" every time, and the task of bringing the goods to land now involved even more difficulty and danger than that of their subsequent distribution, once they were ashore. On 27 September, 1840, the Government cruiser *Harpy*, whilst patrolling in the Channel, made capture of the *Five Brothers*, a smuggling craft belonging to Cawsand, together with seventy-two half-ankers of foreign spirits which had been thrown overboard by the latter in the course of an exciting chase. The remainder of the cargo

[1] *West Briton*, 25 September, 1840.

THE SMUGGLERS

was sunk with large stones "so that the people of the *Harpy* could not recover them"—though it is more than probable that the inhabitants of Cawsand could, and did, since the fishing up of sunken tubs by means of crooks or "creepers" was an art which was well known to the smugglers of this date. In the following week the *Harpy* was successful in capturing, about fifteen miles off the Lizard, another Cawsand vessel, called the *Fox*, having on board one hundred and twenty-six half-ankers of contraband spirit, and four men, including "the notorious smuggler, Peter Benallack, tailor, of Veryan. This," states the correspondent of the *West Briton*, "makes eleven smuggling boats that Lieutenant Drew has taken since he has held command of the *Harpy*, whilst eleven more have been compelled to throw overboard their cargo in order to effect escape when being chased."[1]

The penalty now imposed on the "fair trader" who was caught in the act was certainly severe enough to damp the ardour of all but the most reckless; consisting, as it did, in having his vessel sawn up into three parts. As Commander H. N. Shore has remarked, "the consequent feelings—and language—of the owner, as he watched the slow disintegration of the smart little craft which was the centre of all his hopes, and the source of so much profit, can only be left to the imagination of the reader." Such, however, was the fate which

[1] *West Briton*, 6 November, 1840.

overtook not a few of the Cornish-owned smuggling vessels of this period.

"Last Wednesday week," states the *West Briton*, 24 May, 1839, "the schooner, *Marie Victoire*, laden with coals, entered Falmouth harbour, when she was boarded by one of the preventive men, who, as she had long been a suspected vessel, remained with her whilst she was unloading her cargo off Malpas. The exciseman suspected there was something wrong, but the sailors conducted themselves in such a careless and unaffected manner, as very much to shake these suspicions. On Saturday, however, when a great part of her coal was cleared, the exciseman commenced boring in different parts of the vessel and at length sent his gimlet into a cask of brandy. He immediately sent after the seamen who had gone ashore, but they had effected their escape. The vessel was then brought up to Truro Quay, where it was found she had a false bottom, and that she was well stored with spirits. On Sunday, the officers began to remove their booty, which amounted to two hundred and seventy-six tubs of brandy and Geneva, and the vessel, which was registered in the name of Mr. Jago, of Redruth, is now being cut up. She has been in active operation for nearly three years, and has several times been examined in different ports without any discovery being made."

The sequel to the story is to be found in the brief notice which appeared in the Press some two months later, announcing the "sale of the broken-up hull and boat of the schooner *Marie Victoire*, with her sails and ropes reduced to paper-stuff, and her masts and yards reduced to firewood."[1]

The consequence of such a severe penalty was that the smugglers once again began to change their methods, and instead of risking their own boats, chartered French vessels with which the revenue cruisers had no power to interfere as long as they remained outside of territorial waters. Cruising up and down the Channel during the day, these ships were distinguishable to the smugglers by the cut of their sails, and the farmers also working in the fields kept a close look out for them. In these vessels the goods were brought across, and either sunk near the shore, from whence they could be conveniently "worked"; or else were taken off direct by the local boats which went out to meet them. Dark, moonless nights were, of course, particularly favoured for these operations, and at such times the French ships would draw in close under the cliffs, and a pre-arranged signal having been flashed across the intervening water, the smugglers' boats immediately put off."[2] The number of landing-places along an extensive coast-line, endowed by nature with innumerable coves, inlets, backwaters, and creeks, made detection by the Crown officers very difficult, but it none the less happened on more than one occasion that the occupants of the local boats were surprised and,

[1] *West Briton*, 20 September, 1839.
[2] Stanley Old, *Western Morning News*, 17 January, 1930.

being unable to land without being captured and identified, embarked on the French ship, and spent an unexpected holiday in France before returning to their homes. Occasionally the Frenchmen themselves, by approaching too near the shore, paid the price of their complicity. In December 1838, the schooner *La Vigilante* of Roscoff, with ninety-two tubs of contraband spirit on board, and a crew of six Frenchmen (i.e. Bretons) and two Englishmen, was seized by the coastguards off Carter's Island, near Newquay.[1]

Two years later the French sloop *La Commerce* met with the same fate about a mile off the "Gurnet's Head," to the west of St. Ives, where she was discovered to have one hundred and fifty-eight tubs of brandy in her hold, and a crew consisting of five Frenchmen and one Cornishman, the latter being Philip Light, of Cawsand.[2]

[1] *West Briton*, 21 December, 1838.
[2] *West Briton*, 6 November, 1840.

V

Although, by the middle of the last century, the difficulty of landing goods upon the coast was ever increasing, the facilities for their subsequent distribution through the countryside had reached the highest pitch of efficiency. Once a cargo was safely ashore it could almost always be stowed away within a few hours among the innumerable caves, peaths (wells), barns, furze, ricks or other safe hiding-places belonging to the many landowners who were friendly to the trade. From thence it was dispatched into the interior as time and opportunity allowed. In the eastern part of the county, Millbrook was one of the chief depots for the sale of contraband spirit, which was frequently conveyed into Plymouth in skins, concealed by innocent-looking old market women under their long cloaks.[1] The ancient fishing ports of Cawsand, Polperro, Looe, and Mevagissey were likewise riddled with secret hiding-places, some of which may still be seen in the older houses of these towns to-day.

The smugglers' successes, however, in most cases, involved arduous and exacting toil, and were accompanied by hairbreadth escapes. The goods had to be carried by night, and frequently across

[1] H. N. Shore, *Cornish Magazine*, I, 117.

country over the fields in order to minimize the risk of detection.

"On one occasion," writes Mr. Stanley Old, "a quantity of wines and spirits which had been landed on the coast near Padstow, was 'warehoused' at a farm some three or four miles inland. By some means or other the excise officers had got wind of this and in consequence a raid was expected. It happened, however, that just at this time the farmer's wife was anticipating 'a happy event,' and accordingly the smugglers were seized with the idea of stowing the goods in one of the bedrooms of the house. Immediately after this had been done, the woman retired to bed and the doctor was sent for. Arriving before the search party, the latter at once took charge of the bedroom, into which he forbade the excisemen to enter, on account of the critical condition of his patient. The remainder of the house, however, and the farm outbuildings, were thoroughly searched, but no dutiable goods being found, the party went away satisfied. Exactly how much of the contraband the doctor received for the part he had played is unknown!"[1]

That the smugglers were in the habit of paying in a free-hearted and generous way for the favours which they received, there is no doubt, and this fact in all probability accounts for the affection with which their memory is still regarded. An illustration of this was given to the writer by an old resident of St. Just not long since.

[1] *Western Morning News*, 17 January, 1930.

"The night my youngest sister was born, I can remember we were all sitting up late in the kitchen, and about one o'clock in the morning a knock came to the door. Father got up to open it and found several men standing outside.

"'What's up here, this time of night?' they asked, pointing to the lights in the windows.

"Father explained that a baby was expected.

"'Well,' said the smugglers—for such they were, 'will 'ee 'ave a drop of spirits to cheer yourselves up? If so bring out a bottle and we'll fill 'un for 'ee.'

"Father came in and started looking for a bottle, but not one could be found. The only thing he could lay hands on was one of those great glass carboids, like they use for bringing acid to the mines.

"'Will this do?' asked father, taking it to the door.

"'Aais, all right, my dear,' replied the men—though they must have been a bit surprised at its size. However, they filled it all the same, and then father gave them leave to put a few kegs in his mowy, which was what they wanted. I was a small boy then, but I remember the night clearly enough, and I've got the carboid in the house still, though it's never been filled since!"[1]

Though the profits made by smuggling were generally hard won, the demand for the goods themselves had never been keener than it was some seventy or eighty years ago. At that period, the consumption of a certain amount of

[1] Per Mr. Henry Thomas, St. Just.

alcohol was still looked upon as a necessity even by persons of strictly temperate habits, whilst heavy drinking characterized many households in all classes of society. There are persons still living, indeed, who can remember the time when the small town of St. Ives boasted no less than twenty public-houses, *in addition* to beershops and spirit shops. In all such houses of entertainment "Cousin Jack," as the cognac of the smugglers was familiarly known, found a ready sale, and though the parson and squire sipping their strong waters before the fire in the raging nights of winter might have frowned at the mention of smuggling, they were willing enough, in their secret hearts, to bless the daring men who brought them such liquor at the risk of their lives, and for such absurdly moderate prices. Indeed, the fact that the excisemen's grip was tightening, and that greater daring and cunning were required for the trade now than ever before, only seemed to add spice and flavour to the game. Old ladies sitting at ease in their little parlours over a fragrant dish of tea, knew the joys of smuggling without its risks and hardships, as they handled the rare old egg-shell china cups and whispered to each other: "All smuggled, my dear, like the tay that's in them!"; whilst, in the kiddleywink close by, the miner or fisherman calling for a pint of beer, and seeing a drop of something added to "take the chill off," rejoiced in the knowledge that once again the Cornish boys had outwitted the "sarcher's gang."

THE SMUGGLERS 63

The success of the smuggling trade entirely depended, of course, on the loyalty of all parties concerned, and, true to the Cornish motto of "One and All," it was rarely that this loyalty was ever betrayed. Such cases, however, naturally did occur from time to time. In the village of Shuffley, near Redruth — formerly one of the greatest resorts of the smugglers in the mining districts—one particular family continued to bear until recent times the contemptuous nickname "Informer," in commemoration of the never-to-be-forgotten crime of an ancestor who had betrayed the sacred trust by which almost every member of the hamlet had once been bound.[1]

The quickness of wit and nimble action required by the latter-day smugglers is well illustrated by a story told of a certain quaint old journeyman tailor — Lewis Grenfell — of St. Just. One cold mid-winter day, Grenfell and a companion were engaged in removing a cask of brandy from one of the mine adits which formed a favourite hiding-place for smuggled goods in this district. They had just brought out the cask from the tunnel in question when, as luck would have it, an exciseman was seen approaching. The tailor's companion, thinking discretion the better part of valour, promptly took to flight and hid himself in a thick furze brake near at hand, leaving the other man to face the situation as best he could. In answer to the officer's stern inquiries, Grenfell, who appeared to

[1] Per Mr. William Michell, Redruth.

be shaking with the cold, admitted his offence—indeed, with the incriminating cask beside him he could do no other—but pleaded in extenuation his extreme poverty and the needs of a large family and a sick wife. Finding, however, that pathos produced no effect upon the exciseman, the old man begged only that he might be allowed to taste a drop of the precious liquor to warm his shivering bones. To this the officer agreed, and handed him a gimlet with which to make a hole in the cask. The tailor's hands were numb, however, and his movements so slow that at length the "sarcher," who was also quite ready for a drink, leapt down from his horse and, handing the reins to Grenfell, began "spiling" the cask himself. Hardly had he begun to do so, when the tailor, perceiving his chance, jumped on to the horse's back and made off at a gallop. The officer thereupon gave chase, and scarcely were both men out of sight round the shoulder of the hill, when the tailor's companion crept out from his hiding-place and quickly secured the cask, which, needless to say, the exciseman never saw again![1]

Stories similar to this are, of course, told in many parts of Cornwall. Adjoining a certain farm in the Padstow district there is a narrow lane which takes its winding course down to the shores of the neighbouring bay. On one occasion, a number of years since, the farmer was carrying a keg of brandy through this lane when he was observed from some

[1] Per Mr. Henry Thomas, St. Just.

distance off by an exciseman. The latter, who was on horseback, galloped towards the farmer and fired his pistol as he went, in order to attract attention. Hurrying along the lane, the farmer dropped his load at a certain spot, removed a gate post from its socket, deposited the keg therein and replaced the post, in time to greet the officer as he rode up with a cheery "Good day." In answer to the exciseman's question, the farmer denied all knowledge of the keg, and although the officer was sure that he had seen him carrying it, a search revealed nothing![1]

The smugglers themselves sometimes showed their high spirits by acts of extreme bravado. On one occasion which is remembered by the grandparents of persons still living in the town of Redruth, a band of smugglers rode into the streets by night and stopping under the exciseman's window, called forth in mocking tones: "Would 'ee like to see our 'kags' (kegs), maister?"[2] At this particular period, a certain farm in Gwithian parish was a noted haunt of the smugglers. Passing here on a dark night, the traveller would sometimes find the whole place lit up and numbers of horses and ponies tethered outside. Within the house, meat and drink was going in plenty for all who had a mind to it. Not a word would be said at these strangely convivial parties of the work in hand, and a "sarcher" himself might have mingled with the

[1] Stanley Old, *Western Morning News*, 17 January, 1930.
[2] Per Mr. William Michell.

assembly without being one whit the wiser. Only when the feasting was over, and news had come that the coast was clear, a significant nod from the farmer warned the guests that the time had come for action. Mounting his horse, each man betook himself to a certain spot on the cliffs, where the kegs would be found ready laid. Two of these were slung across the back of each horse and every one rode his way. On one occasion, however, a Redruth man (whose family is still resident in the neighbourhood) was pursued by an exciseman. Reaching as far as St. Erth bridge, he found that his horse was unequal to the burden of himself and the kegs and, accordingly, leaping to the ground, he lashed the animal into a gallop and then ran down and hid himself beneath one of the arches. Not long afterwards, just as he was beginning to feel the water decidedly cold to his feet, he was relieved to hear the thundering hoofs of his pursuer's horse passing overhead. Freed from all further anxiety, he at once came out from his hiding-place and started for his home on foot, to find, on reaching Redruth, that his horse had safely arrived some hours before, together with the precious burden of kegs.[1]

Many are the stories of this sort which are still told of the last days of smuggling, and many more could, no doubt, be brought to light by persons still living were they only considered sufficiently "respectable" for the ears of the modern generation.

[1] Per Mr. William Michell.

"My father, at the age of fourteen," wrote an old gentleman on a recent occasion, "was bound apprentice for the term of seven years to a certain well-known shoemaker in the village in which he lived. The fee required for such an apprenticeship was ten pounds, a great sum of money for poor people in those days, but in return, the shoemaker was required to teach the apprentice his trade, to feed, clothe, lodge him, and pay him sixpence a week, rising to two shillings by the end of his time. My father had good food whilst he was thus apprenticed, but the hours were long—from 7 a.m. to 8 p.m., ordinarily, but on some occasions much longer. The only recognized holidays were Christmas Day, Boxing Day, Feast Monday, and Good Friday, with sometimes a half-day at Truro Whitsun Fair and Summercourt Fair. To vary the monotony of work, however, they often turned out for a night's poaching, also going to Gorran or Portloe, ten miles away, to fetch home smuggled goods—chiefly brandy. This latter was carried in small kegs, slung by a rope over the shoulders. On one occasion, when returning, they espied at some distance a party of excisemen, and were forced to take to hiding in a field of standing corn, where they remained all day beneath a hot sun, with nothing to eat or drink. On arriving home, the liquor was poured into a wash tray and coloured the right shade with burnt sugar, after which it was returned to the kegs and sold to trusty customers."[1]

[1] Reminiscences of Mr. J. C. Hoare, Madron.

Tactful and sympathetic inquiry among the older generation of persons still living in west Cornwall confirms the fact that fifty or sixty years ago, smuggled goods had by no means ceased to find a sale in the county. On a recent occasion, a lady residing in the village of Troon, near Camborne, told the writer that she clearly recollected as a child, how an old woman used to call at regular intervals at her home, offering her parents the chance of purchasing "a little cheap brandy." Where the spirit came from, the old woman refrained from saying, but it is certain that she never lacked customers.[1]

Spirits, of course, were not the only form of contraband dealt in by the smugglers. One day, a man named George Michell drove up at the door of the Angel Hotel at Helston, in a spring cart, the back portion of which was closely covered with a sheet of tarpaulin. "What 'ave 'ee got in there?" inquired the landlady, coming to the door to meet him. "Silk, my dear," replied the man, "do 'ee want to buy some?" "Hush," replied the landlady, "I thoft as much, and what's more there's others know of it. There's a party of sarchers in the bar waiting for you now. They'll be out any minute. What are 'ee going to do?" Without a word the man jumped down from his cart, and throwing the reins to his son, bade him drive into the inn yard. Proceeding himself towards the bar, he greeted the excisemen with a friendly nod.

[1] Mrs. J. Davies, Troon.

"A cold day, gentlemen," he remarked. "What about a drink all round?"

The excisemen, having their man in sight, willingly agreed.

"I expect you found the wind pretty cold crossing Goonhilly Downs this morning," said the officer with a knowing glance; "you come from St. Keverne, I believe. Do you know if there's been much smuggling out that way lately?"

"Aw, ais, pretty fair, I believe," replied the other, "and there would be plenty more if you chaps wasn't always so darned smart. No good for the poor smugglers to try and deceive you. You can see through their tricks every time. It beats me how you do knaw so much."

Between drinking and chatting, the man contrived to spin out a considerable time. Suddenly, however, there was a rumble of cart-wheels and the sound of horse-hoofs outside. One of the men rushed to the window, in time to see an old-fashioned box-hearse being driven out of the inn yard.

"Only a pauper's funeral," he remarked, as he rejoined the others by the fire.

They finished their glasses and then the officer rose and, putting on an official air, turned to the other and said, "George Michell, for that, I believe, is your name, I have a warrant here to search you and the cart in which you drove up just now. I must ask you to accompany me into the yard."

Nothing loth, the other led the way. The

tarpaulin was removed, only to disclose to the "sarcher's" gaze the usual market produce—several baskets of eggs, a few fowls, and some butter.

"Is that all, friends?" inquired the owner, "because, if so, I must be going about my business—and you, I expect, have yours!"[1]

It must be admitted, of course, that such tales as these represent the smugglers' version of the story, and it is necessary, as Mr. Cornish has pointed out, to make some allowances for this when considering them in the light of history. The official records of the custom-houses, however, are not open to the same criticism, and these bear overwhelming testimony to the daring and success which attended the smugglers' activities over a long period of time.

[1] Per Mr. Michell, Penzance.

VI

The end of the smuggling trade, as already shown, did not come suddenly, but its decline, though gradual, was inevitable. As late as the eighteen-seventies, the trade still lingered in some of the western ports. "About this time," writes Mr. William Paynter, "a great deal of rum found its way to St. Ives, being brought there from Holland in a vessel locally known as the *Old Dutchy*. The fishermen used to get the spirit when they were out in their boats at night, disposing of it in the town afterwards with great profit to themselves. This went on for some time, for though the preventive men were suspicious, they had no definite knowledge to work on. At length, they managed to obtain indisputable proof of what was happening by sending spies among the fishermen. The new-comers were very friendly and talkative, liberal with their tobacco, and always ready to stand drinks. As a result, the spies were soon in possession of all the facts they wanted to know. Several houses were raided, and such heavy fines were imposed on the delinquents that they sorrowfully realized that smuggling was no longer a safe or a profitable calling."[1]

With the exception of one trifling incident over a few bottles of scent, little has been heard since of smuggling in St. Ives, or, for that matter, in

[1] *Old St. Ives* (1927), 36.

any other Cornish port. It was but a few months ago that a worthy tradesman, occupying an honourable position in the affairs of his town, told the writer that he believed that his father was the last person to be summoned in Cornwall for smuggling, and added with more than a trace of regret in his voice, "and the last person that is ever likely to be now." A subsequent conversation with an old coastguard commander, whose experience certainly entitled him to speak with authority on the subject, served only to confirm this unromantic point of view. Despite all the very sound arguments which could be put forward in favour of reviving an industry which might help to replace fishing (now, alas! in such poor plight), modern conditions are overwhelmingly against smuggling. Not only has the elaborate organization for the disposal of the goods throughout the countryside been swept away, but the demand for the goods themselves is infinitely less than it was. Whether the coming of the aeroplane will cause a partial revival of smuggling in a different form can hardly be said as yet, but it is certain that the contraband trade itself can never partake again of the romance associated with it in those great days of the past when scores of well-found vessels, and hundreds of honest, daring, reckless men put out from the western ports, and served a sea apprenticeship which made them sailors the like of whom the world will never know again.

WRECKS AND WRECKERS

WRECKS AND WRECKERS

I

FEW aspects of Cornish life have excited more popular interest than the tales of the wreckers, whose misdoings figure so largely in the pages of sensational fiction. At some time or other, every Cornishman, one may suppose, has been asked what his opinion is on this subject, and to such a question an honest man may well be hard put for a definite answer. So much depends on what is really meant by "wrecking." If the latter simply implies a propensity to regard as his own the flotsam and jetsam which the sea casts up upon the coastline, or to be willing at any moment to risk a wet suit of clothes in order to recover such spoil from the waves, then it is probably true to say that the average Cornishman is a wrecker still at heart. To take in thankfulness, however, the harvest which the gods have provided is surely not reprehensible but praiseworthy, whilst the instinctive desire to get something for nothing is one which is scarcely confined to Cornish people.

The writer has in mind an illustration of this which occurred during the war, when the pilot of an aeroplane who had been stunting over a certain Cornish seaside town, at length paid the penalty of his daring by crashing precipitately into the waves. Much to the relief of every one it was soon learnt that the pilot was unhurt, and the genuine concern which had been felt on this head was quickly turned to joy when it was perceived that the machine itself was about to become a "total wreck." By one o'clock in the morning, practically the whole population of the town was assembled on the beach, anxiously awaiting the going down of the tide. Foremost among the crowd were a number of visitors who, corrupted, no doubt, by the Cornish element amongst which they found themselves, nevertheless showed surprising acumen in seizing many of the most valuable portions of the wreck when once the looting began! One remembers in particular a clock which was one of the most coveted of the spoils and which went to an up-country visitor, despite the efforts of a local fisherman who was heard to remark afterwards: "Ais, I had my eye on that, too, but, darn 'ee, the London fellow was too quick. Any one would think he 'd been a wrecker all his days!"

Most people, indeed, have only to experience for themselves the white heat of excitement which the circumstances of a wreck breeds, in order to understand how the Cornishman's reputation in this respect was gained. On such occasions, the most prosaic and respectable people will often reveal a predatory instinct of which they themselves were previously quite unconscious, and in the darkness of the night, with the sound of the breaking surf, and the singing of the gale in one's ears, old

WRECKS AND WRECKERS

instincts and desires will awake to life again in a most surprising way.

Nor are the spoils of wrecking always spurned by those who benefit from them second-hand, as was amusingly revealed by a story told to the writer not long since. During the visit of a lady to the Lizard some forty years ago, a wreck occurred, in the neighbourhood, of a ship which was laden with a cargo of potted goods and other tinned delicacies. Many of the cases in which these were contained came in on to the beach undamaged, and even in those which had been broken by the waves, the majority of the tins were found to be intact. The latter were, of course, soon dispersed throughout the neighbourhood, several of them finding their way on to the table of the friends with whom the lady was staying. This fact caused much distress to her parents who, on learning that the goods were unpaid for, wrote at once to say how surprised they were that such a thing could ever have been countenanced by her hosts. Judging that in such circumstances attack might perhaps be the best method of defence, a parcel containing several more of the offending tins was immediately dispatched by the lady to her parents, with a request that they should first sample the good things for themselves before delivering any final judgment on her conduct. So successful did this procedure prove, that within a few days she received a most cordial letter from her mother, who concluded with a postscript: "Your father and I have much enjoyed the delicious tinned meats which you sent us, and we wonder if it would be possible to obtain any more, if, as you say, every one is doing it, and your friends think that it is *really quite all right*." The story has a no less amusing sequel. For some weeks after the wreck had occurred, the salvage officials were busily employed in removing the undamaged cases to the top of the cliff, an arduous undertaking in which they received considerable help from many of the natives of the district. At length, on a certain day, a sale was called, and dealers came from far and wide, attracted by the likelihood of good bargains. Taking his stand in the midst of the assembled crowd of onlookers and buyers, the auctioneer with a flourish of his hammer announced the terms of the sale, and bade his assistant open the first case, in order to display the excellent condition of its contents. Scarcely had the cover been removed, however, when a gasp of consternation showed that something was wrong, and, drawing nearer, the crowd perceived with mingled amusement and chagrin, that in place of the much advertised goods the contents consisted of nothing but stones! Once again old instincts had proved too strong, and the people who had been so kind in assisting the officials to bring up the cases by day, had been assisting themselves to the contents of the same by night.

For the latter-day Cornishman, wrecking has come to mean little more than a pastime, representing at the most an occasional opportunity of gaining a few perquisites of a more or less illegitimate kind. Very different from this was the businesslike spirit in which wrecking was conducted in the more distant past. From the earliest records which throw light on the subject, it would appear that the right to wreckage in Cornwall was originally vested in the Crown. As may be gathered, however, from various incidents, private landowners began at an early period to make their claims felt in a forceful manner. Thus, in the year 1305, William Le Poer, coroner of the Scilly Islands, arriving in Tresco to inquire into a wreck and to take charge of the salved cargo, found himself seized and imprisoned by a mob, led by the prior of St. Nicholas, from whose clutches he only escaped by buying his freedom at a high price.[1] Shortly after this, on the occasion of a Spanish ship being wrecked on the mainland, the cargo was plundered, and the owner kept in confinement for the space of a year.[2]

As time went on the right of wreck appears to have fallen more and more into the hands of the lords of the coast-lying manors, some of whom possessed very extensive "royalties." Thus, the lord of Connerton, in Gwithian, claimed all the wreck from Cudden Point in Mounts Bay right around the Land's End to Gwithian beach.[3] It is clear, however, that the Crown did not forgo this valuable

---

[1] M. Oppenheim, *Victoria History of Cornwall*, 478.
[2] M. Oppenheim, *Victoria History of Cornwall*, 478.
[3] C. G. Henderson, *Western Morning News*, 21 January, 1929.

right without some show of protest. In '36, Henry VIII, two Norman ships laden with fish from Newfoundland were driven into St. Ives Bay by stress of weather, in a time of war. The townspeople, we are told, seized the vessels, and Sir William Godolphin and many of the gentlemen thereabout came and put the fish into the cellars. The Lord Admiral claimed the ship and cargo as droits of Admiralty; Sir John Arundel also claimed them in right of his Hundred of Penwith. The Lord Admiral issued a citation against the seizure, but afterwards did not prosecute his claim, and the jury determined that Sir John Arundel had most right to the ship and goods, "and so he had them quietly."[1]

Adjoining the claim which was thus successfully defended by the manor of Connerton, came the royalties claimed respectively by the lords of Tehidy, Nancekuke, Tywarnhayle, and Ellenglaze, these together covering the whole of the wreckage along that cruel stretch of coast from Godrevy to Newquay. Going back to Mounts Bay, the lord of Methleigh claimed all the rights of wreck from Cudden Point to Looe Bar, whilst from Looe Bar to Polurrian the manor of Winnianton held sway. Beyond that again came the lord of the manor of Predannack. "The court-rolls of these manors are full of references to wrecks all through the centuries," states Mr. Henderson,

[1] Quoted by C. Bowles, *Short Account of the Hundred of Penwith* (1805).

"and in some cases the value of the commodities which came ashore have never been surpassed except perhaps in the case of the wreck of Prince Charles's wardrobe at Godrevy, during the Civil War." [1]

On 19 January, 1526, a great ship of the King of Portugal, called the *St. Andrew*, freighted with bullion, silver plate, and other treasure, was driven ashore at Gunwalloe by "the outrageous tempest of the sea." Here the vessel became a complete wreck, but, as Francis Person, the King of Portugal's factor, states, "by the grace and mercy of Almighty God, the greater part of the crew got safely to land." Not only were the country people, who had assembled in great numbers on the beach, largely responsible for this, but he adds that by their exertions, which continued throughout that day and the following night, a great part of the cargo was also saved. The latter was extremely valuable, comprising as it did eight thousand cakes of copper, worth £3,224; eighteen blocks of silver bullion, worth £2,250; silver vessels, plates, ewers, and pots, pearls, precious stones, chains, brooches, and jewels of gold; together with a chest of ready money containing £6,240. From further details in the careful inventory drawn up by the Portuguese factor, we learn that the ship was also laden with cloth of arras, tapestry, rich hangings, satins, velvets, silks, chamlets, sayes, and Flemish and English cloth. This was by no means all,

[1] *Western Morning News*, 21 January, 1929.

however, for other curious entries show that there were on board twenty-one hundred barbers' basins, thirty-two hundred latten candlesticks, a great chest of shalmers, and other instruments of music, besides four sets of armour for the King of Portugal, and harness for his horses, etc., the whole amounting in value to about £160,000 in present money. The work of the natives and the crew, however, in saving much of this cargo proved to little purpose. Person, in his declaration, goes on to state that shortly after it was landed, three local magistrates, representatives of the leading families of the district, viz. Thomas St. Aubyn, of Clowance; William Godolphin, of Godolphin; and John Milaton, of Pengersick Castle and the Mount, arrived on the scene with about sixty retainers, armed in manner of war with bows and swords, and made an assault on the shipwrecked sailors, putting them in great fear and jeopardy, and eventually taking from them all they had saved from the wreck. "This," he adds plaintively, "they will not return, although they have been called on to do so." It is true that a very different complexion was given to the affair by the account written by Thomas St. Aubyn himself. In this he states that being in the neighbourhood of Gunwalloe, he heard of the wreck, rode to it and assisted in saving the men; Godolphin and Milaton afterwards joining him with the same object. They found, he states, very little that could be rescued and, seeing that the men were destitute, without money to buy meat or drink, they bought the goods of the ship in lawful bargain with the captain. He further denied any assault, or that they had taken goods to the value of £10,000 from the sailors, adding that, in fact, they had only saved £20 altogether, the bulk lying in the ship still, and that although they had tried to recover more, they had failed even to pay the cost of the labour employed.[1] So the two stories run, but those who have studied the propensities of the Cornish gentry in those far-off days will probably not find it hard to make up their minds which one approximates more nearly to the truth.

At a later date than this, the Arundells of Lanherne (afterwards of Wardour Castle, in Wiltshire) were among those who continued to derive a handsome income every year from the wrecks which occurred all along the Cornish coast. Not only did this great family possess the manor of Winnianton, but also the valuable Liberty of Connerton which, as already described, gave them the right to all wrecks from Marazion to St. Ives. "In addition," states Mr. Henderson, "they had the wrecks near Mawgan Porth and in several other places. At Wardour Castle, built by Lord Arundell in the eighteenth century, the splendid stateroom doors of Spanish oak are said to have come ashore as wreckage on one of the Cornish manors." [2]

[1] Cf. H. M. Whitley, "The Treasure Ship of Gunwalloe," *Journal of the Royal Institution of Cornwall* (1890), X, Pt. 1.
[2] *Western Morning News*, 21 January, 1929.

The "Royalty of Wreck," as may thus be seen, often provided the coast-lying landlords with most valuable perquisites, and it is not surprising, therefore, to find that in some instances the claim to such a privilege was hotly contested. Proof of this may be found in the bitter dispute, which broke out during the earlier part of the eighteenth century, between the Penrose family and the lord of the manor of Methleigh, both of whom claimed the right of wreck between Porthleven and the Looe Bar.

"In July, 1743," writes Mr. Henderson, "matters came to a head when some wreckage, including a cask of salted pork, was washed ashore at Porthleven. Edward Coode, whose father, Samuel, was lord of Methleigh, wearing only his great coat, gloves, and walking-stick, went down to the shore to see that his father's rights were preserved. Squire Edward Penrose, however, appeared on the scene with some men armed with fixed bayonets, who declared that they would shoot the first man who touched the cask. One of them struck Mr. Coode on the breast, and they all appeared to be much in liquor. Squire Penrose seized a musket, and cried, 'Damn him, shoot him, or by God, I'll shoot him.' A great uproar thereupon ensued, but young Mr. Coode managed to escape, and legal proceedings were the inevitable sequel." [1]

[1] *West Briton*, 24 January, 1929.

II

Wrecking, therefore, as may thus be seen, was by no means confined to the lower orders of Cornish society, its greatest and most successful practitioners being those to whom rank and privilege had granted the power to pillage and plunder on a scale undreamt of by the poor. Nevertheless, all classes benefited therein to a greater or lesser degree. When Sir John Killigrew erected the first lighthouse at the Lizard in 1619, he stated that most of the houses in the district were built of ruined ships, and that the inhabitants were enraged by his action, complaining that "I take away God's grace from them, meaning that they shall receive no more benefit from shipwrecks. They have so long been used to reap profit by the calamity of the ruin of shipping that they claim it as hereditary." [1]

As has been pointed out, however, a Killigrew was ever willing to pose as a Christian philanthropist living among savages, when it suited his purpose; as in this case it obviously did. Such sentiments, however, coming from such a quarter, must have caused no little astonishment to a generation whose fathers, at any rate, had known these same Killigrews as some of the most out-and-out pirates that ever sailed the seas. No doubt

[1] Quoted by C. G. Henderson, *West Briton*, 1 August, 1929.

there were people still living at this time who could recall how in 1557, three members of the Killigrew family had attacked a ship off the Land's End and subsequently divided amongst themselves the cargo, which was said to have been worth £10,000. Even clearer in the public memory must have been the exploits of the notorious Lady Killigrew, who, in 1582, had seized a Spanish vessel which was sheltering in Falmouth harbour, removed its cargo to Arwenacke and drowned most of the crew.[1] Perhaps these facts were not overlooked by the Trinity House Brethren; at any rate, the latter refused to assist Sir John Killigrew in his scheme for getting a patent to levy toll on all shipping passing the Lizard, excusing themselves on the plea that the light was useful only as a guide to pirates! In 1680, however, the "brethren" themselves erected the first light tower on the Scillies. Unfortunately, the keepers appointed appear to have been Scillonians who, as Mr. Henderson writes, following Oppenheim and Heath, "used their light to assist, rather than hinder, their relations engaged in the family occupation of wrecking. For over a century the St. Agnes light was a public scandal. Sometimes it shone brightly; sometimes so dimly that it could not be seen from St. Mary's; sometimes it was put out altogether."[2]

[1] *Victoria History of Cornwall*, 490.
[2] *West Briton*, 1 August, 1929. See also Robert Heath, *Account of the Islands of Scilly* (1750), 88. Elsewhere, however, Heath writes: "As to the Scillonians, whom a late author has reflected

This is, in point of fact, the only authenticated statement, known to the writer, which in any way supports the oft-quoted charge, that the men of the west were in the habit of deliberately causing wrecks, and even here, it may be noted, it applies, not to the Cornish people, but to the inhabitants of Scilly! No doubt, however, Parson Troutbeck, who dwelt among the latter, expressed even more correctly the attitude of his parishioners towards wrecking when, as it is said, he added to the litany his famous petition: "We pray Thee, O Lord, not that wrecks should happen, but that if wrecks do happen, Thou wilt guide them into the Scilly Isles, for the benefit of the poor inhabitants."[1] This, no doubt, would quite as truly have expressed the feelings of those who dwelt on the mainland also. Before judging either of them too harshly, however, it would be well to understand something of what that phrase "the poor inhabitants" implied.

Of all the parishes in Cornwall which were addicted to wrecking—and very few of those which abutted on the coastline were not—Breage and Germoe certainly attained to the greatest notoriety in this respect. The district embraced by these two parishes, even to-day, is sparsely cultivated, rocky, bleak, and windswept, and its general

upon for their conduct towards persons shipwrecked on their coast, they are certainly much more known for their services to strangers, in such times of distress, than the Cornish, or any other inhabitants on the coast of England."—*Account of the Islands of Scilly*, 138.

[1] *Cornish Notes and Queries* (1906), 282.

characteristics are sufficient to give some clue to the degree of poverty which must have prevailed among its inhabitants two hundred years ago. Mining at that time provided the parishioners with their sole means of subsistence, but the account books of "Great Work," which during the eighteenth century was the foremost mine in the area, show clearly enough the standard of wages on which a miner and his family had to attempt the task of keeping body and soul together. Between the years 1759–64, the average pay for miners working underground in this district seems to have varied between sixteen shillings and twenty-one shillings a month, from which sum considerable "spales" or fines were often deducted for misdemeanours arising out of the conditions of their employment. Furthermore, when any "lett" or misfortune occurred in the mine in which he was normally employed, the tinner became at once deprived of even this wretched pittance. "We have had the greatest floods of rain here that has ever been seen in any man's remembrance now living," wrote Lieutenant-General Onslow's agent from Gulval on 30 January, 1749, "the tyn-works are all drowned almost and many thousand tynners by that means deprived of employ, and starving, ours amongst the rest."[1] What wonder, then, that to men of this sort, a wreck, with its promise of food for the belly, wine to cheer the heart, and perquisites wherewith to furnish their miserable

[1] See Hamilton Jenkin, *The Cornish Miner*, 169.

hovels, came as a veritable godsend, and that, at the merest possibility of a vessel being driven upon their shore, the tinners would leave their work, and in bands "two thousand strong" follow the same for miles along the coast, trusting only that that Providence which watcheth over all might deem it righteous to deliver the spoil into their outstretched hands.

That under such circumstances, when a wreck actually occurred, small pity was shown by the half-starved tinners towards those who were struggling to escape the fury of the sea, seems more than likely. "The late storms have brought several vessels ashore and some dead wrecks," wrote Mr. George Borlase, from Gulval, 1 February, 1753, "and in the former case great barbaritys have been committed. My situation in life hath obliged me sometimes to be a spectator of things which shock humanity. The people who make it their business to attend these wrecks are generally tynners and, as soon as they observe a ship on the coast, they first arm themselves with sharp axes and hatchetts, and leave their tynn works to follow those ships. Sometimes the ship is not wrecked, but whether 'tis or not the mines suffer greatly, not only by the loss of their labour which may be about £100 per diem if they are two thousand in quest of the ship, but where the water is quick the mine is entirely drowned, and they seldom go in a less number than two thousand. Now 'tis hardly to be imagined," continues Mr. Borlase, "how farr the taking of this infamous practice in its budd, and laying the loss of all wages due and some further penalty on every labouring tynner who should leave his tyn work in order to go to a wreck, would contribute to keep them home and break the neck of it. Next, I apprehend no person should be allowed to attend a wreck armed with an axse or the like, unless lawfully required. They'll cut a large trading vessell to pieces in one tide, and cut down everybody that offers to oppose them. Two or three years ago, a Dutchman was stranded near Helston, every man saved, and the ship whole, burthen 250 tons, laden with claret. In twenty-four hours' time the tinners cleared all. A few months before this, they murdered a poor man just by Helston who came in aid of a custom-house officer to seize some brandy. Next, I humbly apprehend the Bill (then before Parliament to prevent wrecking) does not sufficiently provide against the monstrous barbarity practised by these savages upon the poor sufferers. I have seen many a poor man, half dead, cast ashore and crawling out of the reach of the waves, fallen upon and in a manner stripped naked by those villains, and if afterwards he has saved his chest or any more cloaths they have been taken from him." [1]

It might perhaps be thought that such remarks, coming as they did from the agent of a coast-lying manor with important privileges of its own in regard to wrecking, were to some extent biased

[1] *Journal* of Royal Institution of Cornwall (1881), XXIII, 374-9.

(*See page* 91)

CLEARING A WRECK IN CORNWALL
(after Rowlandson)

By kind permission of Mr. J. A. D. Bridger

against the humbler participants in the spoils. Evidence, however, derived from other sources shows that the writer's accusations of occasional brutality on the part of the wreckers were not without foundation. In 1764, when a French ship was wrecked at Perranzabuloe, not only was the whole of the cargo carried away, but the crew themselves were stripped to their very shirts. Unable to obtain a hearing in Cornwall, the captain petitioned the Crown through the French ambassador, and was eventually awarded compensation.[1]

It must be admitted that the local population were veritable artists in the task of "clearing" a wreck. In 1738, a large ship, the *Vigilante*, from Hamburg, was cast ashore at Perran Uthnoe, in Mounts Bay. Captain Vyvyan who was in command of the soldiers quartered at Penzance, immediately repaired to the spot, but not the least part of the cargo could be preserved, even the sails and rigging being carried away by the country people. Two anchors and nine small guns were all that was saved.

A short while after this, the *Lady Lucy* was wrecked at Gunwalloe, and again the country people did well. A few days after the wreck, five casks of wine were found in the possession of the Vicar of Cury!

By 1748, the soldiers had been removed, and with them all possibility of restraint. In December of that year, the *Alcida*, of Bordeaux, was wrecked

[1] H. O. Papers, 24 September, 21 November, 1764.

at Porthleven, with a cargo of one hundred and sixty-seven tuns of wine. The collector, surveyor, and other officers of the excise arrived soon afterwards, but to no purpose. The violence and brutality of the country people, states the report, were such that they could not save a single cask, and were indeed in danger of their lives. The collector wrote afterwards pointing out how hopeless was their position unless they had troops.[1]

Though the tinners of west Cornwall suffered most in their reputation, they were far from being the only delinquents as regards wrecking. "A ship has just been thrown on the rocks near Looe," states a writer from Liskeard on 20 January, 1750, "seven men and a boy, being all the hands on board, perished. 'Tis said that all the horses in the neighbourhood are taken up about the plunder. Even our town, at eight miles distance, is much depopulated both of men and women—a most melancholy scene."[2] In the following year the custom surveyor at Looe stated that on a ship being wrecked, he endeavoured to form a guard of the townspeople, but that, instead of helping him, they only got out their carts and filled them with the cargo.[3]

Though in the face of all the evidence which exists, it would be impossible to exculpate the

[1] Penzance custom-house books, quoted *West Briton*, 22 October, 1931.
[2] MS. *penes*, Duchy of Cornwall office.
[3] *Gentleman's Magazine*, quoted in *Victoria History of Cornwall*, 508.

inhabitants of the duchy during this century from the charge of practising wrecking to a notorious degree, it is worth while noting that Mr. Borlase, the severest of all contemporary critics, makes no mention whatever of the time-honoured fable of ships being *lured* in on to the rocks. As the writer has said elsewhere, the foul deeds which were done, and they were doubtless not a few, were performed in that white heat of excitement which a wreck breeds, and not as the result of any cold-blooded scheming to deprive others of their lives and property.

Nor is it justifiable in every case to judge the actions of one generation by the ethical code of another. At a time, for instance, when brutality and violence passed for discipline in Britain's proudest service, her Royal Navy, little surprise can be felt if such qualities sometimes informed the actions of those who constituted the lower ranks and orders of the contemporary civil life.

Of all the wrecks which have met their fate on the western peninsula, none is more famous than that of the disaster which overtook Sir Cloudesley Shovel in the year 1707. The event itself is, of course, a matter of history, but so many traditions have gathered around the story, which are illustrative of the temper of those times, that, as Miss Courtney has said, no account of the old sea-life of the west would be complete without it. It was on the afternoon of 22 October, 1707, that the admiral, returning home with the whole fleet, after the capture of Gibraltar, reached the Scilly Isles. The weather being thick and dirty at the time, orders were at first given "to lie-to," but later, about dusk, the fleet again made sail. An hour or two afterwards the *Association*, which carried the commander on board, showed signals of distress, these being answered from several of the others. Two minutes later the *Association* struck on the Gilston rock in Porth Hellick Bay, St. Mary's, and sank immediately, all on board perishing. The *Eagle* and the *Romney* with their crews shared the same fate; the *Firebrand* also was lost, but most of her crew were saved. "The other men-of-war," we read, "with difficulty escaped, by having timely warning." As the result of this disaster, between fifteen hundred and two thousand men and boys were drowned in one night.

So much for the bare facts of history. Tradition, however, affirms that, a day or two before the event took place, a sailor aboard the *Association*, who was a native of Scilly, had persistently warned the officer of the watch, that unless their ship's course was altered, she, with all the fleet, would soon be on the Scilly rocks, amidst the breakers. These repeated warnings, it is supposed, so exasperated the officer that he reported them to the admiral. The latter, vexed that a common sailor should presume to know better than his superiors how to navigate a vessel, gave orders, in accordance with the savage disciplinary methods of those days, that the man should be forthwith hanged at the yard-arm for inciting the others to insubordination. Before his execution, the sailor begged, as a great favour, that the chaplain should be allowed to read him one of the psalms. His request was granted, and he chose the 109th, repeating after the reader in a loud voice the curses it contains, and finally prophesying that the admiral, with all those who saw him hanged, would find a watery grave. Up to that time the weather had been fair, but hardly had the sailor's body been committed to the sea before conditions changed, the wind began to blow, and his shipmates were horrified to see the corpse, released of its winding sheet, following in their wake. Long before the vessel struck, most of the men, it is said, had already given themselves up for lost. According to some of the traditions, Sir Cloudesley's body came ashore on a hatch, on which he had endeavoured to save himself, with his favourite little dog dead by his side. Others relate that, after the wreck, the admiral's body was cast up naked on Porth Hellick beach, where it was discovered by a soldier, who took off a ring which was still on his finger, afterwards burying the corpse in the sands. Yet another account, given on the authority of Robert, second Lord Romney, Sir Cloudesley Shovel's grandson, runs thus: "There is one circumstance relating to Sir Cloudesley Shovel's death that is known to very few persons, namely that he was *not* drowned, having got to shore, where, by the confession of an ancient woman, he was put to death. This she revealed many years after, when on her death-bed, to the minister of the parish, declaring she could not die in peace until she had made this confession, as she was led to commit this horrid deed for the sake of plunder. She acknowledged having, amongst other things, an emerald ring in her possession, which she had been afraid to sell lest it should lead to a discovery. The ring, which she delivered to the minister, was by him given to James, Earl of Berkeley, at his particular request, Sir Cloudesley Shovel and himself having lived on the strictest footing of friendship." "As to the place and manner of his burial," writes Miss Courtney, "all traditions agree. Where he lay (the body was subsequently removed to Westminster Abbey) is still pointed out—a bare spot surrounded by green grass—and the Scillonians will tell you that, because he so obstinately refused to hear a warning and wantonly threw away so many lives, God, to keep alive the memory of this great wickedness, permits nothing to grow on his grave." [1]

[1] M. A. Courtney, *Cornish Feasts and Folklore*, 115-17.

III

Whatever truth there may or may not be in the tradition that Sir Cloudesley Shovel met his death at the hand of a Scillonian, and that this alleged act was inspired by revenge, it must be remembered that English law, as it stood at this time, was a direct incitement to the callous treatment of shipwrecked men. Corpses washed ashore were not allowed Christian burial until about 1808, when a Cornishman, Davies Gilbert, President of the Royal Society, and Member of Parliament for Bodmin, succeeded in getting an Act of Parliament passed for their burial in churchyards at the expense of the parish.[1] Up to this time, the bodies which the sea brought in were buried anywhere and anyhow, in the cliffs, or upon the margin of the beaches, the expense being, in some cases, grudgingly allowed by the lords of the coastal manors. A vivid light is cast on this bad old system by the following letter (quoted by Mr. C. G. Henderson) from the vicar of Breage to the lord of Methleigh, in September 1796: "Dear sir,— By the inclosed paper you will find that the number of dead bodies, and such parts of bodies as with respect to interment should, we think, be

[1] S. Baring-Gould, *Cornish Characters and Strange Events*, 62.

considered and paid for as whole bodies, taken up within the precincts of your manor and buried there after the late unhappy wreck, amounts to sixty-two. The extraordinary charge of two men attending constantly, one of them twelve days, the other thirteen days at 1s. 6d., was thought to be necessary in order to secure the bodies, as soon as they should be cast ashore, from being torn by dogs and other carnivorous animals, and to prepare graves for their immediate reception, being at that time very offensive. This circumstance accounts for the great consumption of liquor, without which the people would hardly have been prevailed with to touch the broken bodies, and also for the pack and rope by which they were drawn up over the cliffs and to the graves. Some of the bodies having been buried where the sand was very loose and shallow, Mr. Tregear was induced to employ four men to hedge the graves about with stones and to lay on large heaps of earth, in order to prevent their being torn up by pigs and dogs. Young Carter's and Laity's journey to Newlyn was not without my advice and approbation. You have the result of their inquiries in the paper respecting the goods that were salved or carried off by the boats belonging to Newlyn and the Mount. . . . It was very unfortunate that your own ill-health and your son's business would not permit either of you to come to the parish at the time. I am well assured that, by proper exertions, goods to a considerable amount might have been secured for you, and even now I cannot but think that enough may be recovered for reimbursing the expenses.

"I remain, dear sir, your most obedient servant,

E. MARSHALL."[1]

Further, English law defined "a wreck of the sea" as anything from which no creature, man or beast, escaped to shore alive. Thus, as has been pointed out, the inhabitants of the district, by their endeavours to save life, were virtually depriving themselves of what might be a valuable prize. Notwithstanding this, evidence shows that the Cornish coast-dwellers often exerted themselves to the utmost in rescuing shipwrecked mariners who were cast upon their shores, even when at the same time maintaining their "rights" with regard to the wreck itself. This is very clearly illustrated by an extract from the journal of that famous eighteenth-century privateer, Commodore George Walker, whose ship the *Boscawen*, as a result of encountering a terrific storm, became a total wreck at St. Ives, on 19 April, 1745. "The people of the sea coast of Cornwall," states the writer of the journal, "have for some years undergone the censure of being savage devourers of all wrecks that strike against their coast. How weak a creature is general belief, the dupe of idle fame! Humanity never exercised its virtues more conspicuously than in this instance in the inhabitants and people of St. Ives. They flocked down in

[1] *West Briton*, 24 January, 1929.

numbers to our assistance and, at the risk of their own lives, saved ours. Mr. Walker would not be prevailed upon to quit the ship till he had seen the sick lifted through the cabin windows into the boats, bidding all, without distinction, provide for themselves, as he was capable of swimming, but he was himself, at last, lifted out by two of the townsmen, strangers to him, who went upon the deck to bring him off. When we came into the town, everybody's house was open to us in all the offices of assistance; but above all other instances which could be given of the generosity of the place, gratitude must here pay her greatest debt in remembering John Stevens, Esq. (of Tregenna) whose unwearied activity, liberality, and prudence in aiding, befriending, and directing our affairs are without parallel, except in other like actions of his own. When we mention this gentleman as most distinguishable amongst others, we do not forget to acknowledge the debt of obligation we owe to the mayor, the magistrates, and other gentlemen of the town, whose invitations, readiness to serve, and other acts of civility rendered them ever worthy the best report of their deserving." The wretched miners, it is true, did not share in the same general commendation, but then, as the writer goes on to explain—"these are a people the civil power is scarcely answerable for, at least for their good manners, as they live almost out of the districts of human society, and may be said to be no visible inhabitants of the earth, though they act in the world. Conscious of this fact, the first night Mr. Walker made all his officers sleep under arms, in order to be in readiness for any attack against the wreck; and accordingly so it happened, for in the night the miners came down and were setting about sharing the wreck amongst themselves. At the very first alarm, the mayor himself was up, and a party of the town who went in arms with Mr. Walker dispersed the crowd, and took some of the men prisoners. The remainder of the time during our stay, which was upwards of three weeks, was solely employed in taking care of the wreck and, through the assistance of the aforesaid gentlemen and others, everything was taken care of with as much exactness as if the wreck had lain at the doors of the proprietors, and a great part was saved to a considerable amount." (*Voyages and Cruises of Commodore Walker*. Edited by H. S. Vaughan, 1928.)

Living as they did under conditions of extraordinary severity and hardship, and deprived of even such civilizing influences as the society of the slightly more educated town-dwellers might have afforded them, it is little wonder that the tinners long continued to bear the worst possible name as wreckers. Courage, at any rate, they certainly did not lack, and not infrequently they paid the penalty for the risks they took, by the loss of their own lives- "The stiffness of the shore adds much to the power of the returning backwater," stated a writer in 1817, describing the wrecking scenes which he had witnessed near the Looe Bar and Gunwalloe, "and it is astonishing with what rapidity the sand is carried away under a person's feet. Once this happens, and he is thrown off his legs, he becomes in jeopardy immediately, and has a very poor chance of escaping unless prompt assistance is afforded. Hence it is that so many persons in the neighbourhood get drowned or have the most hairbreadth escapes when in the course of 'going a-wrecking.' An instance of this occurred but a few years ago when several persons attending a wreck, and not being sufficiently on their guard, were surrounded by the run of a large wave, and four of their number were thrown off their legs and carried away. They were all, however, cast in again by the following wave and three of them, having immediate assistance, were saved. The fourth was floated out once more by an 'out-haul,' which carried him in a sitting posture as regularly and smoothly as though he had been sliding on an inclined plane of ice. In this manner he was hurried into the 'truck' of the waves, from whence, alas! there was no return. At the wreck of the *Resolution* brig at Porthleven, only last January," he adds, "a young man was drowned in an exactly similar way, entirely owing to the dangerous nature of the sand." [1]

Although with the passage of time wrecking began to assume a somewhat less savage aspect than in the past, the practice itself continued far into the nineteenth century. Early in the morn-

[1] Henry Trengrouse, *Shipwreck Investigated* (1817).

ing of Saturday, 4th January, 1817, with the wind blowing at gale force, a brig was observed approaching the then unfinished harbour of Porthleven, in Mounts Bay. When within about two miles of the shore, the vessel came to anchor, and succeeded in riding out the storm until about six o'clock the same evening. At that time, finding that no boat could approach her, and having parted one anchor, the master gave orders to cut the other and ran the ship ashore, this appearing to be the only chance of preserving the lives of the crew. As it turned out, the vessel grounded on a fine, sandy beach to the eastward of the new pier, and the tide having begun to ebb, the crew were enabled to reach the land in safety. No sooner, however, had the tide gone down than the ship itself was boarded by a great concourse of the local population who straightway set about plundering. The whole of the private property of the captain and crew was carried off; the heads of the pipes and hogsheads of wine, which formed a large part of the vessel's lading, were staved in, and kegs and other receptacles filled with the liquor. The arrival of some fourteen dismounted dragoons from Helston, though it must have added a touch of colour to the scene, appears to have served no other purpose, their number being wholly insufficient to restrain the lawless multitude who rushed in from all sides. Out of a cargo of three hundred and seventy-five pipes and twenty-five hogsheads of wine, between fifty and sixty pipes only were saved by the agents. As often happened on these occasions, severe contests took place among the plunderers themselves, each being anxious to secure the largest possible share of the booty. The only casualties, however, appeared to have been a young man of Wendron, who was drowned by the violence of the sea; and two local men who got so much intoxicated with the wine that they were unable to reach home, and perished during the night by the roadside, the weather being very severe at the time. Although the vessel in the first instance had sustained but little damage, by the following Monday she had become a complete wreck, and the country people had ripped up the hull and carried off a large part of the timber.[1]

Some three months later, another brig, the *Mary*, of Ilfracombe, was driven ashore at Fassel Geaver Cove, near Godrevy, in a violent snowstorm and a gale of wind. By a miracle of Providence, the crew were all saved and the captain, assisted by some of the local farmers and the custom officers of the port of St. Ives, succeeded in getting out the necessary cables to hold the ship in a position of safety. During that night and the succeeding day, parties of men were employed about the ship in securing her stores, and keeping watch over what had been saved, with the result that everything was conducted with the greatest regularity, and not the smallest pillage took place. On the second evening, however, a party of Camborne

[1] *West Briton*, 10 January, 1817.

miners arrived on the scene, "determined for a wreck." Within a short time they had cut the ship's cable, carried off two of her small anchors, stolen all the beef and biscuit on board, and even had the hardihood, before it became dark, to steal some of the seamen's clothes, which had been washed for the poor fellows by the people of the adjacent village, and had been hung out to dry. In pillaging the ship they set the watch at defiance, threatening to cut them down with their "dags" or hatchets if they showed the least sign of resistance. The captain who owned the ship and most of the cargo, which was uninsured, was practically ruined as a result of this more than usually infamous conduct on the part of the wreckers, and it is not without a feeling of satisfaction that one learns that the ringleaders were subsequently apprehended and committed to the assizes to take their trial.[1]

Seeing that, during the years 1823–46, no less than one hundred and thirty-one vessels were lost between the Land's End and Trevose Head,[2] a distance of little more than forty miles, the Cornish people certainly could not complain of being bereft of what they had once naïvely termed "God's grace." "I have the honour to acquaint you," wrote Mr. Alexander Shairp to the comptroller-general of coastguards, 4 October, 1838, "that on the 1st instant I received intelligence that a French brig, *Les Landois*, was wrecked between Sennen and

[1] *West Briton*, 28 March, 1817.   [2] Parl. Pap. (1859), X.

Priest Coves. On arriving at the spot, I found the beach covered, for the space of a mile, with the ship's cargo, which the coastguards of the adjoining stations were doing their utmost to protect. The cargo consisted of pipes of wine, casks of brandy, tobacco, cotton, liqueurs, etc. There were four or five thousand people of all classes present, who were engaged in staving in the casks, drinking the liquor and wine, and plundering the property of every description—hundreds of women with pails, pots, jars, and other vessels carrying it off into the country in all directions. We destroyed and upset many hundreds of these vessels in our passage down to the wreck, where we proceeded to protect the full casks which were surrounded by many hundreds of armed men, who threatened to destroy the coastguard, and were armed with staves and pieces of iron from the wreck. It was impossible, in such a case, with our force of twenty-five men, and upon such an extent of coast, to preserve the whole of the property, but, after every exertion had been made, forty-one casks of wine, with a quantity of cotton, cork, staves, etc., were secured and placed in safety for removal to Penzance. . . . The names of some of the parties who committed assault upon the coastguard or in whose possession plundered property was found, have been given to the local authorities but, as some special constables, who arrived late at night, were unable or unwilling to identify the parties who were taken, the number of obstructors, in the execution of this our duty, who have been recognized, amounts only to two, and those with property in their possession to fifteen, which cases are now before the magistrate for further proceedings." [1]

It would be a very great mistake to suppose that wrecking, at this or any other date, was confined to the inhabitants of Cornwall. The report of the Constabulary Force Commissioners of 1839 asserts that on the Cheshire coast hundreds of people were known to assemble on such occasions, carrying off the wine and spirits in kettles or other receptacles. It also describes how, on an Italian vessel being wrecked on the coast of North Wales, the inhabitants robbed the sailors who had escaped from the wreck, and "took the clothes out of their chests before their very faces." Furthermore, we learn from the same source that at Deal, and at other places on the coast of Kent, the country people were in the habit of assembling in such numbers for plundering purposes that the coastguards were sometimes obliged to discharge their fire-arms over their heads before they could be sufficiently intimidated to disperse. Reports of like happenings were also given to the Commissioners from many other districts, including Durham, Yorkshire, Norfolk, Suffolk, the Isle of Wight, Dorset, and Devon. It is true that in most of these places the wrecking consisted chiefly in pilfering small articles of property under cover of darkness, or when the coastguards' backs

[1] First Report of the Constabulary Force Commissioners, 1839.

were turned, and the open conflicts which took place in Cornwall between the representatives of the law and the local population seem to have been rare elsewhere. Furthermore, as the report itself concludes: "whilst in other parts of the English coast, persons may assemble by hundreds for plunder on the occasion of a wreck, on the Cornish coast they assemble in thousands."

IV

By the latter half of the last century, the ever-increasing vigilance of the coastguards was beginning to make wrecking, even in Cornwall, a more hazardous and far less profitable occupation than it had been in earlier times. Like their close confederates, the smugglers, those who continued to indulge in wrecking found that nimble wits and a ready hand were increasingly necessary in order to evade the officers of the law. A story recently told by Mr. Stanley Old, of St. Merryn, is illustrative of this. "During the month of January 1860, a ship named the *James Alexander* was driven ashore by a heavy gale at Porthmeor, near Porthcothan Bay. On board the vessel was found a live pig, for which a general scramble took place amongst the spoilers who had collected from the surrounding countryside. The pig was eventually secured and brought ashore by a man from Penrose. Half-way across the fields, as he was driving the animal towards his home, he was suddenly met by a preventive officer. Now, any one coming from a wreck was always suspected by the officers of being in possession of something to which he had no right, and accordingly the Penrose man was challenged with the words: 'Hallo! what are you up to?' Quick as a flash came the answer: 'There's a wreck out there on the cliffs, and the blackguards have gone and left all the gates open and I have had to round up my stock and drive 'em home.' With a 'Get out, you!' to the pig, the man continued his course, and eventually got the animal safely to his house."[1]

Not infrequently in those days of wooden ships, valuable timber would be washed ashore after the prolonged gales of winter. On one occasion it so happened that large baulks of mahogany had been coming in under St. Merryn cliffs, and several of these valuable prizes had been secured by the farmers of the district and safely hidden in their rickyards. This fact, by some means or other, becoming known to the custom officer at Padstow, the latter journeyed out one evening in order to make inquiries. On his arrival, one of the farmers in question confessed that he knew where the timber was, and offered to take him to the spot where he could see it. Before doing so, however, he suggested their taking a jug of cider, which the officer, after his four-mile walk, was nothing loth to accept. One jug led to another, and it was growing dusk before a start was made. Calling to his labourer to bring a rope and a lantern, the trio set out across the fields to Mackerel Cove, near Trevose Head. On arrival there, the farmer proposed that he and the labourer should tie the rope round the officer's body and lower him down the face of the cliff to the spot where he told him that the baulks could be seen. As already stated, it was by this time practically dark, and as he peered over the

[1] *Western Morning News*, 13 August, 1930.

two-hundred-feet drop, at the bottom of which could be heard the roar and thunder of a heavy breaking sea, the officer's courage completely failed him. Rather than venture his life in such an awful situation, he told the farmer that he would be willing to say no more about it, and with this agreement, which must have proved equally satisfactory to both parties, the inquiry was brought to a close.[1]

Beach-combing, though an unadventurous form of wrecking, sometimes yielded rich rewards to the dwellers by the coast. Gold coinage used often to be carried on ships trading with foreign countries, and when one of these came to disaster, the coins themselves were frequently found upon the beaches for months or years afterwards. In many places, stories are still told of the existence of hoards of gold and silver coins, though unfortunately for the descendants of the people who put them there, the description of the hiding-places seems always too vague to allow of their recovery! It is a fact, however, as Mr. Old has said, that in the past, farms were sometimes bought and paid for in gold currency on such a scale that, if the money had been saved by ordinary methods, the purchasers must indeed have been thrifty. Some sixty or more years ago, masons were called in to make some structural alterations in a large house in the Padstow district. In removing the old plaster from the ceiling of a bedroom, a shower of gold

[1] *Western Morning News*, 17 January, 1930.

coins suddenly descended upon the workmen, and it is said that more than one of the ladies' apron-strings snapped under the weight of gold which was recovered. On the death of the owner of another house in the same district, a relation of the deceased and the housekeeper excused themselves from attending the funeral, on the grounds that it was necessary for them to stay and prepare a meal for the mourners on their return. As soon as the coffin had left the house, the relative told her companion that she was going to make a search, and that the two should go fifty-fifty with the spoils. What they actually discovered is not known, but shortly afterwards the relative, who was married to a ne'er-do-well, who was unlikely to have saved a penny-piece of his own, departed to south Cornwall, where she bought a two-hundred-acre farm and soon retired, as did also her sons at an early age.[1]

Near the church of Gunwalloe, on the shores of Mounts Bay, specimens of the large old-fashioned dollar coins have been frequently recovered by residents in the neighbourhood. These are believed to come from a foreign vessel which was wrecked here in the latter part of the eighteenth century. About the year 1820, the number of these coins which had been found led to the formation of a company, which set about a systematic search in a miner-like way. An iron shaft was made and let down through the sand. The work, however,

[1] *Western Morning News*, 17 January, 1930.

was hindered by the constant gales and rough seas, and soon afterwards the project was abandoned. About the year 1863 another attempt was made to secure the treasure by the employment of divers.[1] This, however, proved equally unsuccessful, but the fact that silver coins are still occasionally picked up on these beaches, shows that the stories told in the neighbourhood are not wholly legendary.

The ill-fame of this district, both as regards wrecks and the lawless character of its inhabitants, lasted far into the nineteenth century. "The dangers of the coast from St. Michael's Mount to the Lizard are too well known to need description," wrote the Rev. G. C. Smith—better known to his contemporaries as "Bo'sun" Smith—in a letter composed shortly before his death in 1860. "Many vessels, especially foreigners from the East and West Indies, South America, and other parts, frequently, in the winter, at night, make the lighthouse at St. Agnes in Scilly, and that on the Longships, off the Land's End, as their first landfall: and if a strong gale from the south-west sets in, they find it impossible to weather the Lizard. They then fall deeper into the bay and are frequently driven, with a violence that nothing can surpass, on to the coast between the Mount and the Lizard. Here they are often dashed to atoms in a moment: or at other times, through the concurrence of some favourable circumstances, are thrown up into places where the greater part of the cargo

[1] Thomas Spargo, *Mines of Cornwall and Devon* (1868).
I

might be saved. Natural depravity and the custom of centuries have inspired the inhabitants of the coast with a rapacity for plundering those wrecks, and the name 'wreckers' applies, therefore, to vast numbers who look for the season of booty. When the news of a wreck flies along the coast, thousands of these people collect near the fatal spot, armed with pickaxes, hatchets, crowbars, and ropes, not for helping the sufferers, but for breaking up and carrying off all they can. The moment the vessel touches the shores, she is considered as fair plunder; and men, women, and children are working on her, night and day, to break her up. The hardships they, especially the women, endure, are incredible. Should a vessel be laden with wine or spirit, she brings them certain death. The rage and fighting to stave in the casks, and bring away the spoil in kettles and all kinds of vessels, are brutal and shocking; to drunkenness and fighting succeed fatigue, cold, sleep, wet, suffocation, and death! Once last winter, a wreck happened on Sunday; they had everything ready and sallied forth, not, however, until the clock had struck twelve at midnight, when all checks of conscience were thought to be removed. Five hundred little children in a parish are brought up in this way, and encouraged by precept and example to pursue this horrid system. The practices of these wreckers have, by one severe instance, awakened the attention of the Bishop of St. David's, who lately exhorted his clergy to preach everywhere against it. To this method may be added, with as great effect, the persuasion of those who will visit their cottages. It appears for the credit of the county, however, that these practices are confined to a few western parishes, *and that even there, no deeds of personal inhumanity towards the unhappy sufferers have been permitted in modern times, even by the plunderers themselves.* Inheriting from their ancestors, however, an opinion that they have a right to such spoils as the ocean may place within their reach, many even among the more enlightened inhabitants secure whatever they can seize, and conclude without any hesitation that nothing but injustice, supported by power, and sanctioned by law, can wrench it from their hands." [1]

The fame of Bo'sun Smith, it may be well to recall, rested upon his power as a popular preacher and, like many another of his kind, he was gifted, in no small degree, with the histrionic art. The scenes, therefore, which he depicts, though doubtless not without foundation, cannot be assumed in all respects to constitute a literal presentation of the facts. Less sensational, but probably far truer to type, is the picture given by Mrs. Bonham in her book, *A Corner of Old Cornwall*, which recalls more intimately than any other of its kind, the state of life which obtained in the isolated Lizard promontory in the earlier part of the last century. That the people were "wreckers," the authoress makes no attempt to disguise, but her account

[1] Quoted by C. G. Cooke. *Topographical Description of Cornwall.*

entirely dispels the illusion that the majority of the wrecks were attended by such scenes of drunkenness as the former writer has conjured up. Indeed, the reverse seems to have been true since, in certain cases, wrecks were the means of introducing to the people teetotal drinks of a kind which they had formerly scarcely known. "Many useful things are stowed away in the cottages after a good wreck," writes Mrs. Bonham. "The 'tea-wreck,' in particular, was a wonderful piece of good fortune for folks, very few of whom could ever indulge in such an expensive luxury. There was also the 'coffee-wreck,' when many tasted that delicious stimulant for the first time."

Of all the "useful" wrecks of this sort which have occurred on the coast of Cornwall, none has better reason for being remembered than that of the *Good Samaritan*, which came ashore at Bedruthan Steps on 22 October, 1846 — a year before the Trevose Lighthouse was completed:

> The *Good Samaritan* came ashore
> To feed the hungry and clothe the poor,
> Barrels of beef and bales of linen,
> No poor man shall want a shillin'.

The vessel, whose untimely end gave rise to this well-known panegyric, was bound from Liverpool to Constantinople with a valuable cargo of silk and cotton goods. The night on which the disaster occurred was an unusually wild one, and the vessel was dashed to pieces and completely destroyed within a few hours after she had struck. Out of her crew of ten, two only survived the horrors of the night. The gale, as not infrequently happens, was succeeded by glorious weather, and next morning crowds of people from all the surrounding countryside were gathered on the beach. Nothing remained of the wreck itself but the pieces of smashed-up timber and her bottom, which lay embedded in the sand close to what is now known as the Samaritan Rock. The cargo, contained in iron-bound bales, many of which had burst, lay scattered around on the sands, whilst strips of the finest silks and cotton hung waving in the breeze from the topmost points of the rocks, on to which they had been tossed by the sport of the waves. "Looting," writes a local resident, "was carried on incessantly. Never before, or perhaps since, have the ladies of the neighbourhood been clothed in such rich silks and other fineries. After the wreck, excise officers searched practically every house in the district, where much of the spoil was discovered and its possessors arrested. It is said that at the time Bodmin gaol was half full of St. Eval men. In many more cases, however, the officers were outwitted. News quickly spread when a search was in progress, and in one house where a cupboard was crammed chock-full of material, the kitchen dresser was placed in front of it, and although the premises were searched, the finds were nil!" Amongst those who did well out of the wreck was a certain George Lee, of St. Merryn, a noted character of his day, concerning whom many stories of wrecking are told. In his younger days Lee had been in the navy and, as an illustration of his vigorous constitution, it is said that when his ship was in Plymouth, he would think little of walking the fifty-odd miles during the night in order to reach his home. On the occasion of the wreck of the *Samaritan*, it is recorded that George Lee, whilst working in partnership with a boon companion, discovered a quantity of gold coins. The cliffs at Bedruthan Steps are nearly four hundred feet high, and then, as now, there was only one track leading up from the beach, and this was guarded by a preventive officer. How to get past the latter was the question that had to be solved. Eventually, it was decided that the gold coins should be transferred to Lee's pocket, after which the pair separated, his companion, Northcott, going straight to his home, there to await Lee's arrival and the sharing of the spoil. This was done; but actually, it was many hours that Northcott had to wait before his partner arrived. When he did so, Lee presented a sorry spectacle. With clothes covered in mud, he informed Northcott that he had been attacked and robbed, his pockets and their contents having been cut clean out of his clothes. "This tale," states Mr. Old, "was evidently believed by Northcott and others; but," he adds, "it is a significant fact that soon after this affair George Lee was in a position to buy a cottage and the adjoining meadow."[1]

[1] Stanley Old, *Western Morning News*, 17 January, 1930.

V

Though many of the tales and incidents related above might seem to reflect small credit on the character of the Cornish people, it would be a very unjust statement of the case which made no attempt to show the reverse side of the picture. For if the dwellers by the Cornish sea have harvested for long centuries where they have not sown, they have time and again given of their best with an unstinting hand. Nor is this only true of latter days, when the lifeboats of Cornwall, manned by their gallant crews of local fishermen, have done such signal service to mariners passing these storm-vexed shores. As long ago as 1802, when according to popular conception the average Cornish coast-dweller was still the brutal wrecker, dear to the heart of the novelist, local records show that the bulk of the population were none the less ready to risk their own lives in the attempt to save those of the chance strangers whom Fate had made dependent on them for aid. "On Thursday last," states the St. Ives correspondent of the *Cornwall Gazette*, 6 March, 1802, "there was driven on shore in this bay, by a violent gale of wind at north-east, the ship *Suffolk*, of London, laden with bale goods and rice from Bengal. She came on shore in a shocking and distressed condition, having split all her sails to pieces the night before, the ship leaking badly, and of the twenty-one hands on board, six only able to do duty, the rest being sick. The crew remained on board in a perilous situation for some hours; but by the vigilant exertions of the people from the shore (*who always in such cases distinguish themselves by manly alacrity*), boats were got from the creek of Hayle, and another large eight-oar boat was *carried* from St. Ives (three miles) by land, which being well manned, attempted at all hazards to get to the ship. In the meantime the captain and crew on board fastened a line to a keg, and let it drift to the shore, and the boat's crew, having got hold of it, by that means hauled all the people, one by one, to land, except two who were so ill as not to be able to struggle, and who accordingly died in their hammocks. The weather the next day proving favourable, the bale goods, consisting of raw silk and muslins, with some hundreds of bags of rice, were brought to St. Ives by boats; and yesterday the ship itself, with part of the cargo, was brought into St. Ives pier much damaged."

In the year 1817, a similar wreck occurred at Gunwalloe Cove, near Helston. Here again conspicuous bravery was shown by the local population in rescuing the sailors who had jumped overboard amidst the heavy breakers. Among the rescuers was a certain William Triggs, of Mullion, who, perceiving one of the less fortunate sailors surrounded by the waves, and being carried out in an exhausted state by the violent "undertow," rushed into the surf, and succeeded in getting hold of the man by the sleeve of his coat. "They were now," states an eye-witness, "both off their feet, and beaten and tossed about by the surf. Perceiving this, the people who had the end of the rope which was about Triggs's waist, being eager to get them both to land, hauled on it somewhat violently. As a result, the sailor's coat rent, and the piece coming off in Triggs's hand, the latter was hauled in to the beach without the other man. Another young man, however, a farmer named John Curtis, observing the mishap, immediately dashed into the water, and by his gallant action, succeeded in bringing the sailor to shore in safety, though at the peril of his own life." [1]

Some ten years before this, there had gone ashore on the Looe Bar, a short distance southward of Gunwalloe Cove, H.M. frigate *Anson*, among the most famous of all the wrecks which have occurred on the Cornish coast, and worthy, as results proved, to be regarded as one of the outstanding events of British maritime history. The *Anson*, forty-four guns, had left Falmouth on Christmas Eve, 1807, for her station off Brest, as a look-out ship for the Channel Fleet. A gale from the west-south-west having sprung up shortly after her leaving port, she continued to be buffeted about for some days in the seas off Mounts Bay, and at length, on the 28th, the wind still increasing, the captain determined to put back to Falmouth. Owing,

[1] Henry Trengrouse, *Shipwreck Investigated* (1817), 84.

however, to mistaking the Land's End for the Lizard, the ship became embayed, and at the cry of "Breakers ahead!" from the man on the lookout, both cables were let go. The *Anson* rode to these till the morning of the 29th, when they parted, and the captain, in order to save as many lives as possible, decided to beach her on the sands off the Looe Pool. "By this time," as the Rev. Baring-Gould has written, "a tremendous sea was running, and as she took the beach, only sixty yards from the bar, she was dashed broadside on, but happily for those on board, heeled landwards. Seas mountains high rolled over her, sweeping everything before them." The captain, realizing that no chance of rescue was possible for those who remained on board, gave orders to the men to save themselves as best they could. Whilst a small proportion succeeded in fighting their way to safety through the boiling surf, the majority of those who leaped over the side were instantly swept off their feet by the terrific "undertow," and carried out into the trough of the waves, never to return. In consequence of this, though the wreck lay under the very eyes of the crowd which was gathered on the beach, upwards of a hundred men are believed to have been drowned, including the captain, who stood by the frigate to the last.

In the meantime, those who had got to shore reported that two women, and a like number of children, were yet remaining on board. On learning this, to the lasting honour of Cornwall, several local men, including Mr. Tobias Roberts, of Helston, and Mr. Foxwell, of Mullion, determined to give their own lives, if necessary, in making the hazardous attempt to reach the ship.[1] In this act of almost unparalleled bravery they succeeded; but at what risk and peril to themselves may be judged from Mr. Foxwell's own statement. "I went into the surf as far as I could," he writes, "and got so near the ship as to have a child handed to me, and Mr. R—— at the same time had one handed to him. I carried the child under one arm, and held by the rope with the other. Mr. R——, though I begged him, refused the assistance of the rope. After a few moments, however, a tremendous wave broke in upon the beach, so we were both enclosed by the waters. As I was holding by the rope, I sustained myself, but Mr. R—— was washed off his legs. I saw his danger, but feared if I quitted the rope, I should get into the like difficulty. My apprehension, however, for his safety, and that of the child, prevailed and I ran the risk (being a tall man), and seized him by the collar, and succeeded in getting him upon his legs again, otherwise I do not doubt that both he and the child would have been drowned." [2]

Whilst these agonizing scenes were taking place, there was standing amongst the crowd of spectators on the beach a certain Henry Trengrouse of Helston, whose subsequent devotion to the cause

[1] S. Baring-Gould, *Cornish Characters and Strange Events*, 60–1.
[2] H. Trengrouse, *Shipwreck Investigated* (1817), 21.

of life-saving, were it but one-half as famous as it deserves to be, would surely atone for all the sins which have been attributed to his countrymen in the pages of popular fiction. By one of those curious chances of fortune, however, which ever seem to deprive the true inventor of his recognition and reward, Trengrouse's service to humanity in the evolution of the rocket apparatus is still almost unknown to the world at large. And yet, in actual fact, it is to him, above all others, that the world is indebted for the invention which has since saved many thousands of lives and which is now a commonplace to all who dwell by English shores. From the day of the wreck of the *Anson*, it is said that Trengrouse's mind never ceased to be exercised by the thought of how some means of communication might be established between vessels and the shore, and throughout the remainder of his life he freely sacrificed his money, business, and health, in the effort to achieve, and to get others to adopt, the substance of his grand invention. Something of the same idea, it is true, had occurred to Lieutenant John Bell in 1791; and in 1807 Captain G. W. Manby had carried the proposal a stage farther by experimenting with a mortar for throwing a shot, with a line attached, to stranded ships. Manby's mortar, however, notwithstanding that its inventor was rewarded by the Government with a sum of £2,000, was cumbrous and dangerous, and after several men had been killed during tests, it was definitely abandoned by the authorities. The superior advantages of Trengrouse's apparatus are too manifold to be discussed in detail, but it will suffice to point out that the rocket apparatus, being much lighter than the mortar, could be readily carried to situations on the cliffs whither it would have been well-nigh impossible to have conveyed the latter. Moreover the velocity of a rocket, increasing gradually, was much less likely to cause the breaking of the life-line than a mortar, whose action was so sudden and violent as frequently to snap the rope by the force of its discharge. In addition to all this, Trengrouse's rocket could either be fired from the shore to the ship or vice versa, and had the added advantage over a shot, of showing its track by a trail of fire, thus rendering it visible to the crew and their rescuers at night time when wrecks most commonly occur. It was Trengrouse's earnest desire to see every ship supplied with a rocket apparatus, since vessels being almost invariably wrecked *before* the wind, the line might the more easily be fired from a ship than from the shore. For years, however, Parliament continued to haggle over the matter and little was done. Nevertheless, the ardour of the inventor survived every discouragement, and his last words to his son as he lay on his deathbed on 19th February, 1854, were: "If you live to be as old as I am, you will find my rocket apparatus all along our shores." The prophecy has, indeed, been fulfilled, and the world of to-day is still benefiting from the achievement for which

Trengrouse had sacrificed his all. In return for the outlay on his experiments, however, of over £3,000, the inventor received only two money grants to the value of £50 and thirty guineas, together with a silver medal and a diamond ring. Even the latter, which had been presented to him by the Czar of Russia in recognition of the services which his apparatus had rendered in saving shipwrecked lives in the Baltic and the Black Sea, Trengrouse had been constrained to pawn, in order to carry out the further investigations for which his own country was not sufficiently grateful to pay![1]

[1] See S. Baring-Gould, *Cornish Characters and Strange Events*, 63–7.

VI

Meantime, however, the gallant work of rescuing shipwrecked lives went on. Numbered among the many disastrous wrecks which have occurred on the Scilly Islands was that of the steamer *Thames*, which went ashore in a violent gale in the year 1841. Immediately the discovery of the wreck had been made, we learn that boats began putting off from the islands, despite the imminent danger from the tremendous seas which were running. "Indeed," wrote an eye-witness, "the distress on land appeared to be almost as great as that on the vessel, for crowds of women were out on the hills bewailing the anticipated fate of their nearest relatives. It should further be recorded," he adds, "to the lasting honour of the islanders, that although in the course of their task they frequently fell in with various parts of the cargo (such as casks of porter, whisky, etc.), they gave not a moment's thought to securing these as objects of salvage. Their sole meritorious object was to render prompt and efficient aid for the preservation of life." [1] Those who escaped from the sea, moreover, found that the islanders were as generous as they were brave, the latter, despite their own poverty, putting

[1] Rev. G. Woodly, *Narrative of the Loss of the Steamer "Thames" at Scilly* (1841).

everything which they possessed at the service of the shipwrecked passengers and crew.

In the pages of an old diary kept by a resident at St. Ives, during the years 1806-48, many other instances are recorded of the bravery of the local population. Under the date 24th December, 1838, the writer notes: "A very heavy gale from northwest to north-east with thick rain. At 1 p.m. a vessel was seen running in for Porthmeor beach, but, by hoisting a flag on the island, she hauled to more, and came round the head and let go her anchor at the back of the quay. The anchor, however, not holding and it being low water, she struck, and the sea made one complete breach over her. Two light seine boats were manned in attempt to rescue the crew, but being struck with a heavy sea were thrown so far to leeward, that they were obliged to run them on shore on Porthminster beach. A tow-boat was next manned, but filled with water by being struck with a heavy sea. A gig got near, but was struck with a sea and filled. The tow-boat was again manned with a fresh crew, a sea again filled her and washed two men out of her. She was a third time manned, when they succeeded in rescuing the crew. Afterwards the vessel beat in near the rocks on Porthminster beach, but was got off by the pilots the following day (Christmas) on the flowing tide."[1]

On 7th April, 1840, the sloop *Mary Anne*, of Poole, in the course of a heavy gale from the north-east,

[1] Diary in the possession of Col. T. J. Chellew, St. Ives.

split her sails, and in running for the pier at St. Ives was struck by a sea on the Ridge. As a result of this, she became unmanageable and shortly afterwards went on shore under the "Mills." The lifeboat was manned, but owing to bad seamanship was likewise thrown on shore. By a most daring attempt, however, on the part of two local fishermen—Sam Uren, jr., and R. Welch, jr.—who swam out to the vessel through the sea, a line was eventually got on board, and by this means the crew, consisting of the master, one man, and a boy, were hauled to shore in safety. On 24th August, 1842, the writer of the above-quoted diary notes: "Heavy gale north-north-east. At 1 a.m. a large barque discovered in the bay. The quay light was put in, and a tar barrel burnt at Cairn Crowse. The vessel wore and made for the light. The *William* gig succeeded in boarding her after great risk of their lives in getting over the Ridge (it being low water), and brought the vessel to an anchor to the eastward of the Carrack. Proved to be the *Bosphorus* for Jamaica, with a general cargo. Pilotage claimed £400, settled for £150." [1]

The last sentence of this entry throws an interesting light on Cornish character. Willing to risk all at the moment of danger and prepared, as he is, to gamble his own life on the chance of saving those of others, the typical Cornishman sees no reason why he should not drive the best possible bargain once the crisis is over. The profits of pilotage were in

[1] Diary in the possession of Col. T. J. Chellew, St. Ives.

some cases very considerable. On 28th February, 1838, two St. Ives boats, who managed to bring in a French brig which had been abandoned off the Land's End, were awarded £1,000 for their services by the Admiralty Court. A year later, some Newlyn and St. Ives boats received £450 for salving the derelict *John*, of Sunderland. On another occasion, the St. Ives pilots demanded £120 for bringing in the French brig *Normand*, of Cherbourg. After a good deal of haggling, they were at length granted £100, as a result of the captain's own statement that it was fully due, although as the writer of the diary naïvely adds, "had they been offered £50 or £60 at first it is very likely it would have been accepted"! In some instances, however, the pilots overreached themselves in their demands. On 8th November, 1838, the French barque *Joséphine*, which had been brought up by the Scilly pilot, was handed over to the charge of the St. Ives men. The latter anchored in the bay that night, and the next morning slipped the cables, warped her in, and demanded £170 for their services! This was, not unnaturally, refused by the owners; and the court before whom the case was brought, considering the charge to be a shameful one for so trifling a matter, gave the pilots nothing, and ordered them to pay their own costs.[1]

Although it might perhaps be claimed that the profits of salvage and pilotage were, in some cases,

[1] Diary in the possession of Col. T. J. Chellew, St. Ives.

sufficient to inspire the coast-dwelling population with motives for service which were not wholly disinterested, there is no such charge which can ever detract from the heroism of the crews who have manned the lifeboats. As Mr. Claude Berry has finely written in his foreword to the story of Cornwall's oldest lifeboat station which passed its centenary a few years ago: "No hundred years has been more crowded with daring deeds, acts of supreme courage and self-sacrifice than the century of lifeboat service which has elapsed since the founding of the first Cornish station at Padstow in 1827. No distressed vessel within sight of the cliffs ever sought help from the lifeboat and was denied it. Sometimes, within the space of twenty-four hours, Padstow lifeboatmen have been out on three distinct services. Twice their lifeboats have been wrecked—on one occasion five men being drowned, and on the other every man of the crew perishing in the sweeping waters. But the great work of life-saving has continued, and to-day our lifeboatmen are as ready as their splendid predecessors to man the boats when precious lives are in danger."[1]

What is true of this particular station, is true of all. "Never shall I forget," wrote an old inhabitant of Penzance on a recent occasion, "the wreck of the *North Britain*, a barque of seven hundred tons which, when homeward bound from America, got lost in a fog and went ashore on the Eastern Green. It was on a Sunday afternoon,

[1] *The Story of Padstow's Lifeboats.*

early in December 1868, and a terrible day it was, with the wind blowing a hurricane. As soon as the signal went, hundreds of people were swarming down on the beach, and very soon by their aid the lifeboat was got out; Higgins as usual in the bow, and Tom Carbis steering. There were no engines, of course, in those days, and the boats had to be pulled through the water by oars. However, they managed at length to struggle through the terrific seas until they got quite close to the wreck when, all of a sudden, a great wave struck the lifeboat, and over she went with the crew underneath. Somehow, they managed to struggle out, and by a superhuman effort righted her. No sooner had they done so, than another sea struck her and over she went again. Once more they got her on to her keel, and all except one man struggled aboard. He was called Hodge, and a wave carried him away from the boat. He tried to swim ashore in his cork jacket, and how we were thrilled when a man named Desraux rode out amongst the breakers on horseback and hauled Hodge in by the collar! The lifeboat then gave up the attempt to reach the wreck, for the crew were so exhausted by their experiences as to have scarcely strength to pull ashore. As soon as she was beached, however, a volunteer crew was called for, and, despite the fact that what had happened to her before had been clearly visible to those on the beach, she was quickly manned and launched again. In the meantime, the crew of the barque, thinking that their chance of rescue had gone when the lifeboat capsized, had lowered their whaler. This was smashed to pieces almost immediately. They then got out their jolly-boat, filled her with men and began to row ashore. They had got about three-quarters of the way in, when she was up-ended by a sea and the men were flung out. Spectators waded into the water as far as they dared and pulled some ashore, but four of the sailors were drowned. Those who remained on the barque, however, were saved, for the volunteer lifeboat crew managed to get to them." [1]

A plain record of facts, told in a plain unvarnished manner, this story is characteristic of countless others which illustrate the heroism of the crews who man the lifeboats of the Cornish coast. Although the introduction of wireless and the passing of the sailing ship have happily rendered wrecks a much less frequent occurrence than formerly, still, when the worst comes to the worst, and vessels are driven landwards to their fate, the lifeboats are out on their work of humanity, and the gallantry which distinguished their crews in the past is being perpetuated by their descendants of to-day. These matters are well known to all those who dwell within sight and sound of the Cornish seas; but it is none the less an ironical fact that for the world at large, the deeds attributed by fiction to the wreckers of long ago still excite more attention than all the life-saving by which their sins have surely been atoned.

[1] John Richards, *Western Morning News*, 13 January, 1930.

THE FISHERMAN'S TRADE

THE FISHERMAN'S TRADE

I

THE smuggling days of Cornwall are over and past, and the wrecker of history and romance has become the mere gatherer of driftwood upon her beaches, but still the fisherman plies his ancient trade, the first of all the long-shore types to take to the sea for a livelihood, the last to leave it.

To visit a port like St. Ives in the fall of a winter's afternoon, and to watch the herring fleet as it goes streaking out across the darkening waters of the bay, is to recapture something of the spirit of the old sea-life of the past. True, the days of mast and sail are over, and the throb of petrol-engines has replaced the creaking of ropes in the pulley-blocks and the strain of canvas tautening in the wind, but the appearance of the men on deck in their heavy oilskins and great sea-boots, or the proud and anxious women who, with shawls gathered about their heads, stand watching them off from the end of the granite quays, has little changed in all the centuries of similarly enacted scenes which such ancient ports have witnessed.

It has been truly said that of all those who have followed the sea for a livelihood, the fisherman has had least glory and most toil. In the cold bluster-nights of winter, with the salt spray freezing his hands and limbs to the very marrow, the fisherman still spends in labour the hours when others sleep. Out in their tiny boats, or in undecked "gigs," the latter exposing their crews to all the rigours and hardships of wind and rain, they know, as few landsmen ever can, what the struggle for existence means on the open sea. Some have paid the penalty of their calling, even within the most recent years, by being swept overboard when their hands have become too numbed with cold to grasp the means of safety. Others, again, have gone to their fate when returning to port, full-laden with the harvest. Often enough at such times, no sound or cry has been heard above the roaring of the wind, only the sudden disappearance of one of the gleaming lights has warned those who were following that a boat had foundered. Though friends might be not far off, slender indeed are the chances of rescuing those whom the sea engulfs in the blackness of the night, when never a shout may be heard, and a sinking man may see his last hope of deliverance pass by but a few yards distant from his eyes. Or, again, in the thick and dirty weather, when the mist and rain come down and hide the very lighthouse beams, how many a fisherman must have seen, in his mind's eye, the blackness of the "Stones," and the jagged reefs where the deep-sea weed floats upward on the swell of a rising wave, or sinks again to hang in horrible festoons before the gulfs where conger lie, and where the waters suck and moan, like vampires awaiting the dead. For though the fisherman, like his comrade the miner, may be a man of few words in regard to danger, he is gifted with all the imagination of the Celt, and when in conversation he speaks of some spot or other as being an "ugly plaace in a ground say" (sea), his words suffice, for those who know him, to conjure up visions of danger more fearful than those described in any work of fiction.

Despite all the changes of a mechanized world, therefore, the fisherman's life is a hard one still, dependent, as he is, not only on the unforeseen chances of Nature in the prosecution of his work, but on the verdict of others for the ultimate reward of his toil. For, in the simple, hard-working share-fisherman of the west, striving to maintain himself in the possession of his own boat and tackle, may be seen one of the last outposts of an older order of individualism engaged in an heroic struggle with the massed forces of the highly-organized economic world of to-day. Out in his boat at night, perhaps, whilst riding beneath the stars, the fisherman may almost forget the thraldom in which he lies; but, with the return to port in the morning, any dreams which he may have had of being still his own master are quickly shattered. For between him and the consumer of his catches, the middlemen now stand, masters of his fate, no less than of the countless town-dwellers who might, but so infrequently are permitted to, benefit from the cheap food which the fisherman's labour should provide. When fish is scarce in the ports, the price is good, and herrings may fetch as much as sixteen shillings a hundred (120 in reality) for those who have them to sell. At this price the buyers are clearly able to make a profit or they would not give it. The next night, maybe, the fishing is more general, and, with fairly large landings, the price sinks, perhaps to eight shillings. Shortly after this, the whole fleet of sixty or more boats may return to port one day heavily laden with an abundant harvest, which has to be "given" to the buyers for two shillings and sixpence per hundred or even less. In the meantime a box of one hundred and twenty herrings may be sent to London for approximately two shillings, so that, assuming the price of the fish in the shops throughout the country to average twopence each (a very modest estimate!), it would appear that of every £1 worth of herrings consumed by the public after a large catch the chain of middlemen will receive fifteen shillings and sixpence, in comparison with the fisherman's two shillings and sixpence.

Were the problem to be presented to them thus, the middlemen would, of course, point to their overhead charges, such as cellar rents, and the like, which have to be met, be the quantity of fish landed great or small. This, however, is a mere begging of the question, seeing that the same conditions apply equally to the men who have to pay not only for the purchase of their boats, nets, and gear, and the instalments on their engines (which are rented), but to provide the running expenses of petrol and oil, to say nothing of their labour which is performed under conditions of such hardship and peril. Indeed, of the two, the fisherman's overhead costs are the more constant, for the latter has still to meet the upkeep of his boat and its running expenses whether he catches any fish or not, whereas in the case of the buyers, the railway freights which, as they never tire of pointing out, constitute their heaviest charges, are variable, being less in proportion when they are dispatching large quantities of fish, and obviously not being incurred at all when they have none to send.

As things stand at present, therefore, owing to the inadequacy of the price which he receives when his catches are good, and the heavy losses which are frequently incurred when the fishing is poor, the share-fisherman, whose luck has once been against him, sinks deeper and deeper into the slough of insolvency, finding himself in the unhappy position of neither receiving the living wages of a hireling nor a proper participation in the profits of independent ownership. That the system whereby the fish, for which he has risked his capital, and in some cases even his life, and has in return been paid a farthing, should be sold in a shop round the corner for twopence or twopence-halfpenny, is all wrong, the share-fisherman has no doubt; but failing to see any solution to this problem, he has developed an attitude of fatalism which renders the organization of any co-operative method of selling extremely difficult. His children, however, are growing up with the fixed determination that they, at any rate, will no longer endure the hardships which their fathers face for such an inadequate return, and so, year by year, the inshore fishery is dwindling, and a valuable part of the nation's food supply is being strangled at its source.

Formerly the actual work of selling the fish occupied more time than it does to-day, with the result that many of the fishermen, after being out all night, were detained at the auctions until almost midday. By the time, therefore, they had returned home and had dinner, it was necessary for them to be getting ready to go to sea again, so that in the busy part of the season many of the fishermen never took off their clothes or got a regular period of sleep from Monday to Saturday. Small wonder, then, that, apart from any religious consideration, the fishermen of Cornwall have so earnestly striven for the preservation of Sunday as a day of rest, realizing, from their own experience, the human wisdom which underlay the Old Testament command.

The St. Ives fishermen in particular can claim to have shown for at least three centuries that they have been willing to observe the Sabbath even to their own hindrance. In 1622, we find a minute recorded in the borough accounts to the effect that "no owner of boats or nets shall dryve or sett their nets or owners of seines row to stem the Sunday night or any time befor day of that night," under penalty of a fine of ten shillings for each owner and three shillings and threepence for each fisherman. That this regulation was strictly enforced, is proved by the entries for money received for Sabbath-breaking which appear in subsequent pages of the same accounts. Moreover, such lapses when they occurred were always severely criticized by the leaders of local society. In a scarce little volume recording the life of Thomas Tregosse, of St. Ives, a seventeenth-century Puritan divine, we read that in the summer of 1658, "the fishermen taking a great number of pilchards on a Saturday, all the night was spent in saving of them, and the seamen were very intent in drying their nets on the Lord's day. This, Mr. Tregosse rebuked them for, withal giving them to understand that they provoked the Lord deservedly to withdraw His blessings from them, which happened accordingly. For from that time to the end of the fishing season they had not another opportunity of employing their nets."[1]

In 1827 the Sabbath was still being observed with all its former strictness, and we learn from an old diary that on 12 August of that year "two shoals, by colour, passed out, but no 'Hevva' (cry, proclaiming appearance of a shoal) it being Sunday." In 1831, the seine owners renewed their agreement not to catch fish on the Sabbath day, and, in

[1] Quoted by Mr. C. G. Henderson, *Western Morning News*, 19 September, 1929.

consequence, although on 28th August of that year immense quantities of pilchards passed through all the stems, close to the rocks, one small shoal actually coming inside the quay-head under the seine boats, "no one attempted to catch them (it being Sunday)—until the evening, when Mr. Tremearne caught five hundred hogsheads at Porthminster." The temptation, indeed, must have been strong, and it is small wonder that the fishermen sometimes partially yielded to it, as in this case. On Sunday, 16 October, 1836, five seine boats at St. Ives again shot their nets, "but only one reaped any benefit." During the next year, the diary records: "*Tantivy* shot on an immense body of fish, but the men did not obey the huer and the fish were lost. The *Francis* then shot on the same shoal, which when taken was supposed to be from four to five thousand hogsheads." Apparently this occurred on a Saturday, for we read that "the seine being so full, they were obliged to shoot another outside it on Sunday." The results, however, do not seem to have justified the Sabbath-breakers, for the diary adds, "it is supposed two to three thousand hogsheads must have escaped and died, immense piles of dead fish washed ashore every day, and carted away as manure by the country people." In 1838, a large body of fish was again discovered on a Sunday morning, close to the point at Carrack Gladden. "The finders immediately made hevva, but *no notice was taken*. Charles Tremearne then ran home to St. Ives, when all the boats were immediately manned; but . . . the fish had gone!"[1]

A year later, another incident occurred which was no doubt regarded by many of the fishermen as a Divine intervention. "On Sunday se'nnight," states the *West Briton*, 15 November, 1839, "a man employed as a huer (watcher) to one of the seines at Newquay, ran to the neighbouring church to inform the gentleman who superintended the seine in question that the bay was full of fish and to rally the crew that might be assembled there. Not being a very frequent attendant at the church himself, the huer had much trouble in finding the agent, but at length, after searching the different pews, he espied him to his great satisfaction, and delivered the glad tidings. They both left the place immediately, followed at full speed by a long train of persons whose curiosity had been excited. But lo and behold! to their great surprise and disappointment, when they arrived at the cliff there was no fish in the bay, whilst the huer had forgotten to keep the boats afloat!"

[1] From an old diary in the possession of Col. T. J. Chellew, St. Ives.

II

The mention of fishing regulations at St. Ives in the early seventeenth century proves that the industry is of no recent growth. Its beginnings, however, though certainly dating from a period many centuries before this, are impossible to define. Prior to the Norman Conquest, as Mr. Howard Dunn has pointed out, the difficulties of obtaining salt for curing must have kept the trade in fish within very narrow limits. Though there is evidence of small quantities of salt having been obtained by the evaporation of sea water ("salt works" are mentioned in Domesday Book), the common method of preserving fish was by sun-drying. Only those fish which carry their fat in their livers were thus "curable," and the method was not applicable to pilchards or herrings whose fat is contained in their bodily tissue.[1]

Early in the thirteenth century, however, King John granted licences to merchants of Bayonne to fish "for whales, conger, and hake, from St. Michael's Mount to Dartmouth," and this association with France brought French salt into the country, as well as better material for nets than that provided locally.[2] From this time onwards,

[1] Cornwall "Education Week" Handbook (1927), 108.
[2] Cornwall "Education Week" Handbook (1927), 108.

the fishing industry of Cornwall and Devon began to prosper, until, under Tudor administration, it had assumed a position of national importance. During the reign of Elizabeth, the Council of State itself set about formulating a mass of petty regulations with the two-fold object of encouraging the development of the industry, and "the conserving of the profytable foode (fish) for the liege people of the realme." In respect of the latter, the orders were primarily concerned with the best means of distributing the fish. Thus, in 1588, it was ordained that of the pilchards taken at Cawsand Bay, "two parts should be distributed among the towns of Plymouth, Milbrooke, etc., and one-third at Cawsand." Needless to say, the complications which arose out of such orders were endless; and, from the first, they were generally evaded by the inhabitants of Cawsand who, besides knowing something about fish, and the length of time which it would keep, were determined, for pecuniary reasons, to salt in their catches on the spot, and make better prices by exporting them overseas. Such an idea, however, was abhorrent to Elizabethan government. In 1590, came another order requiring that "all shadds, cellars and pentises, called 'Linns,' which had been erected since 1588 should forthwith be plucked down." It was stipulated, however, that if after the requisite two-thirds of the fish had been brought to Plymouth, "it have not a ready sale within fowre tydes, it shall then be lawful for the seynars to carrie the same away by water or land to anie other place within the same counties, but in no sort to carry or sell the same beyond the seas." [1] As the fish had generally gone bad by this time, this concession seems to have awakened little enthusiasm among the merchants. Oblivious of this fact, the council proceeded in a fatherly manner to explain that the principal intention of the order was not, as might well have been supposed, to put difficulties in the way of trade, but "to preserve the use of this kind of fish called pilchards, to serve for the food of the people of the said counties, and not to be for private gaine carried out of the realme to strangers and to defraude the naturall inhabitants of their profytable foode. Moreover," the council continued, "it is not meant but when it shall please God to grant encrease of the same kind of fish, more than sufficient to serve the necessities of the people of the realme, upon signification thereof to the Lords of the Council by the Justices of the Peace of the same county, etc.—leave may be granted to export the same." [2]

With this somewhat indefinite assurance, the more law-abiding merchants and fish-curers had presumably to be content, but there were obviously many others who continued to evade the regulations, esteeming their own profit above their country's weal.

The Government, however, did not merely

[1] Acts of Privy Council, 1590-1, 137-42.
[2] Acts of Privy Council, 1590-1, 137-42.

confine its attention to restricting the exports of fish, but showed that it was willing to extend its paternal care to the industry by stimulating the consumption of the former in the home markets. Amongst the various steps which were taken to this end, the most important, perhaps, was the continuing of the national fast-days, long after the religious significance which had attached to them in pre-Reformation times had passed away. It has been calculated that during the Elizabethan period there were no less than one hundred and fifty-three days in the year on which it was officially forbidden to eat meat.

Nevertheless, despite all the efforts of the Council of State, the development of the fishing industry of Great Britain, apart from that of Devon and Cornwall, still left much to be desired. The chief reason for this seems to have lain in the curious prejudice or apathy which caused the herring fishery to be almost completely neglected by English fishermen, who were content to allow the Dutch to come over to their very shores in the pursuit of this fish, and afterwards to sell it to English buyers for handsome prices. "All these herrings the Dutch do catch in the Yarmouth seas," wrote a pamphleteer in 1614, "they sell for ready money or gold to the Yarmouth men that be no fishermen, but only merchants and ingrossers."[1] The result was that when Carew

[1] "England's Way to Win Wealth." See Arber, *English Garner*, IV, 333.

published his *Survey of Cornwall* in 1602, the ancient fisheries of Cornwall and Devon were still of much greater importance than those of the eastern counties. From a muster of ships and mariners made in the year 1582, it appears that Cornwall had a sea-going population of nearly two thousand, which was slightly exceeded only by that of Devon. The next two counties, Norfolk and Suffolk, claimed but sixteen hundred and twelve hundred respectively, so that altogether the mariners and fishermen of Cornwall and Devon exceeded those of the two eastern counties by more than a thousand.[1]

This preponderance is partly accounted for by the fact that the herring was much less neglected in the west, where the fishermen were not only accustomed to take large catches of these fish upon the coast but, by the beginning of the seventeenth century, at any rate, had begun to follow them as far afield as the shores of Ireland.[2] The chief cause, however, of the flourishing state of the west-country industry lay, as already shown, in the valuable monopoly which it enjoyed of the pilchard, a fish whose taking and curing continued until recent times to be the mainstay and support of the inhabitants of the Cornish coast.

These fish, which Carew describes as being "the least in bigness, greatest for gaine, and most in number," were formerly wont to reach the Cornish

[1] Sir William Monson, *Naval Tracts*, ed. Oppenheim, 188.
[2] Hobson Matthews, *History of St. Ives*, 339.

shores "betweene harvest and Alhallon-tyde," when their coming was eagerly awaited by all classes of the population. They were taken by two different methods, known to the fishermen as "driving" (or drifting), and "seining." "The drovers," writes Carew, "hang certain square nets athwart the tyde, thorow which the schoell of pilchards passing, leave many behind intangled in the meashes. When the nets are so filled, the drovers take them up, cleanse them and let them fall again."[1] Straightforward and innocuous as such a method sounds, it nevertheless caused infinite contention, the seiners complaining "with open mouth" at the drivers' short-sighted greed in thus breaking up and scattering the shoals of fish before they reached the shore, where they might be taken in far greater quantities by the use of the seine net. This dispute, long, loud, and violent, as subsequent history proves it to have been, continued to vex the minds of the local population until, at length, the time came when both seiner and drifter alike were overwhelmed by their common enemy—the trawler.

A "sayne," in Carew's time, commonly consisted of three or four boats carrying about six men apiece, "with which, when the season of the year and weather serveth, they lie hovering upon the coast, and are directed in their works by a balker (Dutch *balken*, to shout) or huer who standeth on the cliffe side and from thence best discerneth the

[1] *Survey of Cornwall.*

quantitie and course of the pilchard, according whereunto he cundeth (as they call it) the master of each boate by crying with a lowd voice, whistling through his fingers, and wheazing certain diversified and significant signs with a bush which he holdeth in his hand. At his appointment, the sayners in the boats cast out their net, drawing it round to either hand as the schoell lyeth, beating with their oars to keep in the fish (as the ends of the net were being drawn together) and at last either close and tuck it up in the sea, or draw the same on land with more certain profit, if the ground be not rough of rockes. After one companie have thus shot their net, another beginneth behind them, and so a third, as opportunitie serveth. Being taken, some, the countrie people, who attend with horses and ponies at the cliffes side, in great numbers, doe buy and carrie home; the large remainder is, by the merchant, greedily and speedily seized upon." [1]

To those who have themselves watched the "shooting" of a seine, this brief, but strikingly vivid account of a scene which must often have been witnessed by the writer near his home at East Antony three hundred years and more ago, shows clearly enough how little the methods of this particular branch of the fishing industry were destined to change. On many a high look-out along the Cornish coast may still be seen the "huer's hut," or "balking-house," wherein, until

[1] *Survey of Cornwall.*

recent years, patient watch was kept for the great shoals of pilchards which once so regularly enriched these shores. Hanging within such huts, might be seen the "bushes," consisting of wooden hoops covered with white bags, and the long tin speaking-horns or trumpets, by means of which the modern huer "cunded" or signalled to the boats which still lay "hovering upon the coast." It was not until the year 1924, in fact, that seining was at length brought to a close at St. Ives. In 1928, the last of the seine boats was sent to the Scilly Islands, the whole of the remainder of the great fleet once possessed by this port having been ruthlessly broken up for firewood. The bushes, trumpets, and other paraphernalia from the balking-house were fortunately preserved, and are now in the possession of the St. Ives Old Cornwall Society.

Before entering upon a description of the all-important seining industry, however, and showing how much the latter formerly meant to Cornwall, it is desirable to glance back once more on another early development of west-country fishing, which proves that as long as four hundred years ago the inhabitants of these areas were willing to risk even the hazards of an Atlantic crossing in the pursuance of their calling. For it is indeed an astonishing fact, and one which has scarcely received the notice which it deserves, that within less than thirty years after the voyages of Columbus and Cabot to the American continent, the hardy fishermen of Devon and Cornwall had already embarked on that most exacting of all sea enterprises—the great Newfoundland trade. As early as the year 1527, we read of the little Devonshire ships being unable to carry home more than a portion of their huge catches derived from this source.[1] On 20 July, 1594, Sir Walter Raleigh wrote to Sir Robert Cecil pointing out that certain "great Spanish men-of-war" had recently given chase to several British vessels as far as Dartmouth. "It is likely," he adds, "that all our Newfoundland men will be taken up by them if they be not speedily driven from the coast for, in the beginning of August, our 'Newland' fleet are expected, which are above a hundred sail. If those should be lost, it would be the greatest blow ever given to England."[2] Two years later, another correspondent, writing to Cecil from Plymouth, states: "There is arrived in these ports within these fourteen days past, to the number of fifty sail, this country shipping, all laden with Newfoundland fish which, as it is thought, will be laden away by Flemmings and Frenchmen that have their ships here ready for the same."[3]

By the early decades of the seventeenth century, as many as two hundred west-country vessels were engaged in the Newfoundland trade. In

---

[1] Newfoundland Fishery.—*Encycl. Brit.*
[2] Hist. MSS. Comm. (Salisbury). Report IV, 566.
[3] Hist. MSS. Comm. (Salisbury). Report V, 387.

THE FISHERMAN'S TRADE

1626, the number dispatched from Devonshire alone was estimated at one hundred and fifty, whilst, in Cornwall, the ports of Saltash, Looe, Fowey, Mevagissey, Falmouth, St. Mawes, St. Keverne, Penzance, St. Ives and Padstow were all taking their share in the great adventure.[2] Every year, hundreds of west-country fishermen signed on, and shipped away for a period which involved two summers and a winter of separation from home, and a life of indescribable hardship. Down to about a century ago, many ships, locally manned and built, still annually sailed from Devonshire to the Newfoundland shores. The principal ports concerned during this period were Dartmouth, Teignmouth, and Exmouth, the central recruiting station for these being at Newton Abbot. Here, according to a recent correspondence in the *Western Morning News*, many agreements were formally signed at the local hostelries, being afterwards clinched with cider, beer, or rum — and not infrequently all three.[3]

Quite apart from the special rigours of the Newfoundland trade, the toil of the fishermen generally during the sixteenth and seventeenth centuries was subject to a variety of hardships and perils which now seem scarcely conceivable. "Poor, painful fishermen," Monson calls them, "who get their living with more pains, with more

[1] Newfoundland Fishery.—*Encycl. Brit.*
[2] *Victoria History of Cornwall*, 491.
[3] *Western Morning News*, 21 March, 1929.

cold and watching than any other trade or people whatsoever; but," he adds, "indeed their greatest danger is interruption by pirates."[1]

During the period of the wars with Spain, the kidnapping by the enemy of west-country fishermen was a favourite method of attempting to gain information concerning the doings of the English fleet. Actually, the value of such a policy to the Spaniards would appear to have been extremely doubtful since, judging by the depositions of those who were allowed to return, they generally contrived to bring back as much information as they could ever have given. Nevertheless, the practice long continued. Thus we read that in June 1595, one Sampson Porth, of St. Keverne, whilst fishing with three others in Falmouth Bay, "was taken by a shallop of Bluett," and brought before Don Diego, "who, by an Englishman that was in one of the galleys, examined them on oath as to what preparation of shipping was being made in England."[2] A year later, another Cornishman, Richard Perne or Peren, of Penryn, was likewise seized by a Spanish galleon as he was out fishing by night, and carried away to Spain, where he was held captive for the space of six months.[3] Nor were such incidents confined to the western parts of Cornwall. In 1599, Richard Carew informed the Privy Council "that yesterday four ships and a

[1] Monson, *Churchill's Collections*, Vol. III, bk. vi, p. 497.
[2] Cal. S.P. Dom., 1595-7, 59.
[3] Cal. S.P. Dom. 1595-7, 172.

pinnace came before Plymouth harbour and took five fishing boats and most of their men." [1]

So far from ceasing at the conclusion of the war with Spain, these terrors increased tenfold. When Englishmen would probably fain have had peace, others had learnt their piratical ways of war, and the "Dunkirkers" had begun to harass British shipping. On 31 December, 1600, William Stallenge wrote to Sir Robert Cecil, from Plymouth: "The Dunkerk's men-of-war remain about the Lizard, where they have taken divers ships and barks, taking out their principal men and suffering the rest to depart." [2] By 1608, it was estimated that there were five hundred sail of pirates in English waters.[3] Shortly after this, the Algerian and Sallee rovers began to make their appearance in the Channel. In 1625, Penzance was petitioning for a fort "because of late terribly terrified by the Turks." [4] In the following year it was stated that the Turkish men-of-war were sighted daily off the shore, "so that no fishermen dare go forth." [5] In 1631, the inhabitants of Fowey stated that their town was "so decayed in shipping, mariners, fishermen, and all sorts of people living by trade, being spoiled by Turks and pirates, and daily sustaining infinite other losses at sea, that through poverty many people have abandoned the town

[1] Cal. S.P. Dom., 1598–1601, 188.
[2] Hist. MSS. Comm. (Hatfield House), X, 431–2.
[3] Cal. S.P. Venetian, 1607–10, 192.
[4] *Victoria History of Cornwall*, 495.
[5] Cal. S.P. Dom., 1625–6, 370.

and gone to other places to seek their living." [1] Five years later, it was reported that fifteen fishing-boats belonging to Looe and Helford had been taken within a month.[2] In the same year, 1636, Edmond Percivall wrote to Sir Phillip Percivall: "I advise you to send no more cattle over (to Ireland) whilst the Turks are so busy, lest both your cattle and your gentlemen should suffer, there having been a multitude of passengers taken this summer. Sir Francis Godolphin and his lady and his servants, with his brother Captain Godolphin and his wife, going to the Isles of Scilly, some three or four leagues off the shore, were taken by the Turks, and one of the Turks attempting to abuse the captain's wife, he presently ran him through, whereupon they cut him in a hundred pieces, and they carried Sir Francis and the rest away captives. God of His mercy send us some relief." [3]

Such were the perils under which the local seagoing population laboured, until the time came when the Sallee men and Dunkirkers were at length driven out of the Channel by the very efficient Commonwealth navy.

[1] Duchy of Cornwall Records, per Mr. R. L. Clowes.
[2] *Victoria History of Cornwall*, 495.
[3] Hist. MSS. Comm. (Egmont Papers). Quoted by "Lanje," *Western Morning News*, 27 January, 1931.

III

From this time onwards, the fishing industry continued to make great strides. That there were fluctuations, of course, goes without saying. Tonkin, at the beginning of the eighteenth century, noted that at times when fish was scarce upon the coast, the fishermen might often be seen lying about basking in the sun for weeks together "rather than earn a penny at husbandry, though their wives and children were starving at home."[1] In another period of great scarcity towards the end of the same century, Maton describes how the fishermen of Fowey and their families were reduced to such straits as to be dependent on limpets and other small shellfish gathered from the rocks as their sole means of support.[2]

On the whole, however, the fishing trade, and, in particular, the inshore seining for pilchards, developed on a tremendous scale during the course of the eighteenth century. "This fish" (i.e. the pilchard), wrote Doctor Borlase in 1758, "comes from the north seas in immense shoals, and about the middle of July reaches the islands of Scilly and the Land's End of Cornwall. The pilchard continues off and on in the south channel,

[1] R. Carew, *Survey of Cornwall* (edit. 1811), 35 n.
[2] *Tour of the Western Counties*, I, 143.

principally from Fowey harbour westward, and is taken sometimes in great numbers at Mevagissy, in the creeks of Falmouth and Helford harbours, at St. Keverne and in the Mount's Bay, as also in St. Ives Bay and the northern channel.[1] With the taking this fish by seine-nets and drift-nets, the curing of them with salt and exporting them to foreign markets, the world is so well acquainted that I need only suggest in a summary manner the advantages of this fish to the county of Cornwall —it employs a great number of men on the sea, training them thereby to naval affairs; it employs men, women, and children at land, in salting, pressing, washing, and cleaning the fish. In making boats, nets, ropes, casks, many other trades are dependent on the same; the poor is fed with the offal of the captures, the land with the

[1] The pilchards were taken throughout three stretches of the coast. The first extended east of the Lizard Point to Bolt Head in Devonshire, a second area was included between the Lizard and Land's End, whilst the third area was centred around St. Ives. It was common for one of these districts to be full of fish, whilst in neither of the others was a "school" to be seen, but towards the end of the season the fish often changed from one area to another. —J. Couch, Royal Cornwall Polytechnic Society, Report 1835, p. 70. After about 1840, the pilchard fishery of the south-eastern extremity of Cornwall greatly declined, whilst in the St. Ives area, where in Dr. Borlase's day it had been of less importance than in the other two, the seining showed a rapid increase in development.—J. S. Courtenay, Royal Cornwall Polytechnic Society, Report 1838, 121. In 1877, St. Ives was by far the greatest seining centre of the county, possessing no less than 288 seines. It is doubtful, however, if half this number were in actual use.—Royal Cornwall Polytechnic Society, Report 1878, p. 98.

"Bulking" Pilchards in a Fish Cellar

(See page 177)

refuse of the fish and salt, the merchants find the gain of commission and honest commerce, the fisherman, the gains of the fish. Ships, likewise, are often freighted hither with salt and into foreign countries with the fish, carrying off at the same time part of our tin." [1]

During the ten years 1747–56, the total quantity of pilchards dispatched from the four principal Cornish ports—Fowey, Falmouth, Penzance, and St. Ives—averaged thirty thousand hogsheads, or ninety millions of fish, annually, and the value of these, including the extracted oil and the Government bounty of eight shillings and sixpence on each hogshead, was estimated at approximately £50,000 a year,[2] a very great sum, considering the value of money in those days. In 1790, after several years in which the seining had been practically a failure, the fisheries produced fifty-two thousand hogsheads; whilst in 1796, the quantity of pilchards taken exceeded sixty-five thousand hogsheads. The huge catches of this year surpassed all the expectations of the merchants, and Gilbert notes that "such was the scarcity of salt, the fish-owners were obliged to send several vessels to France for a sufficient quantity to cure the fish that were taken." [3] It is quite clear, however, that the catches of 1790 and 1796 were exceptional, and between the latter year and 1802, the normal

[1] *Natural History of Cornwall*, 273.
[2] *Natural History of Cornwall*, 272–3.
[3] See J. S. Courtenay, Royal Cornwall Polytechnic Society, Report 1838, 118–19.

M

exports varied between thirty to forty-four thousand hogsheads per annum.[1]

The Reverend J. Skinner, who made an extensive tour through Cornwall about the year 1798, estimated the initial cost of a seine, with its full complement of boats and nets, at approximately £1,000, and he states that each seine employed an average of nineteen hands. In addition to these, at least five thousand persons, of whom four-fifths were women, were engaged in salting, packing, pressing, and preparing the fish; whilst ropemakers, blacksmiths, shipwrights, and sailmakers to the number of over four hundred, and not less than one hundred and fifty female "twine-spinners," found subsidiary employment in catering for the needs of the industry. In all, some six hundred nets were commonly made during each winter season. As regards wages, the same writer states, "the men at Newquay have seven shillings a week, and one quarter of the net proceeds of the fish and oil. The general sum obtained by the men, exclusive of their wages, is from £15 to £25 each for the season. The expense of curing a hogshead of fish is from a guinea to twenty-three shillings, of which charge the cost of salt alone is six shillings. The fish have lately sold from thirty-five to forty-two shillings per hogshead."[2] Whilst this price was in advance of the average obtaining forty years earlier—estimated by Borlase at thirty-three shillings—it probably did not

[1] *Cornwall Gazette*, 31 July, 1802. [2] Brit. Mus., Add. MSS. 28793.

represent any great difference in real money, as the cost of living had risen rapidly during the latter decades of the eighteenth century.

The fishing industry, moreover, then as now, was subject to those wild fluctuations, both in regard to prices and in the quantity of fish taken, which have ever tended to make the fishermen's livelihood a most precarious and uncertain one. The home market for pilchards has always been extremely limited, and from early times the greater part of this fish has been exported to Italy, where, as a writer once humorously remarked, "they enable the Holy Father and his Catholic children to keep their Lent, by filling their bellies and fasting at the same time."[1] Herein lies the explanation of the once popular Cornish toast:

> Here's a Health to the Pope! may he live to repent
> And add just six months to the term of his Lent,
> And tell all his vassals from Rome to the Poles
> There's nothing like pilchards for saving their Souls!

"Long life to the Pope, death to our best friends, and may our streets run in blood" was another favourite toast which illustrates the same point.

The principal ports of delivery for pilchards were Genoa, Leghorn, Civita Vecchia, Naples, Venice, and Trieste, and great numbers of small Cornish-owned vessels were employed in carrying the fish thither and in bringing home fruit, olive oil, and other miscellaneous cargo. As may well be imagined, correspondence between the local fish merchants of the past and their Italian

[1] *Cornwall Gazette*, 31 July, 1802.

customers often presented considerable difficulties, a fact which is clearly shown by the following letter from Mr. Antony of St. Ives, to Bernadina Polomba, of Civita Vecchia:

"11 October, 1779.

"SIR,—I received your favour of 13th ult., and am surprised you should write me in such bad language as I cannot make sense of, particularly that letter of 26 July, and that of 9 August are so writ as not to be well understood. I mentioned to you in my letter of 4 September desiring you would get some friend to write your English letters; as I cannot comprehend the true meaning of those I have received, how is it possible to understand so unintelligible writing. Yours of 21 December, 1778, was a well wrote letter, from which you gave me encouragement to correspond with you, this your favour of 13 September, I cannot rightly understand. This is the third I have received writ by a novice who do not understand English." [1]

It was perhaps as well for the Cornishman's reputation that the recipient of this letter was *not* a very good judge of English, or it might perhaps have occurred to him that Mr. Antony's own epistolary style was susceptible to some improvement. Still less, apparently, did it ever occur to Mr. Antony that *he* might have found a friend to write his Italian letters!

In time of war, the overseas market for pilchards was, of course, greatly restricted, with the result

[1] Formerly in the possession of Sir Edward Hain, St. Ives.

THE FISHERMAN'S TRADE

that prices slumped, and the fishermen became deprived of one of their principal sources of revenue. In 1801, ten thousand hogsheads of pilchards were sold at St. Ives for manure, at tenpence per cart load, owing to lack of other sale.[1] "Last season, before the peace (of Amiens)," states the *Cornwall Gazette*, 31 July, 1802, "the price of pilchards per hogshead was as low as twenty-eight shillings. The glad tidings of peace, however, immediately raised it to forty-seven shillings. The number of seans afloat this season on the coast of Cornwall exceeds two hundred, and the value of this dead property amounts to £160,000 (at £800 per sean), exclusive of the current expense of wages which, at eighteen men to each sean at seven shillings per week per man, is £1,260 per week more." Penzance alone had thirty-six seines afloat in the following month, with a complement of sixteen men to each, and nearly a hundred and fifty driving boats which carried three or four men apiece. The seiners here received wages of about ten shillings a week, and the huers a guinea, besides a small percentage of the fish taken.[2]

Whereas the seines were owned in almost every case by parties of "adventurers," who were commonly merchants or men possessed of substantial property, the driving boats or drifters were usually the property of the more respectable

[1] "Notes on Pilchard Fishery," Royal Cornwall Polytechnic Society, Report 1878.
[2] *Cornwall Gazette*, 7 August, 1802.

fishermen themselves. The latter, accordingly, received no wages, their remuneration being entirely dependent on the success or otherwise of the season's fishing. Such profits as were made, were divided into eight shares, of which one was set aside for the upkeep of the boat, three for the nets, the remaining four going to the men. The master of the boat claimed no more than one of his crew, but the boy who usually formed one of the latter, was held to be sufficiently rewarded with the fish that fell into the sea when the nets were drawn. In order to secure this portion, which was sometimes considerable, he was furnished with a bag-net at the end of a rod, known as a "keep" net.[1]

In a good year, such as that of 1802, the share-fishermen were said to be gaining as much as eighteen shillings a week. The quantity of fish on the north coast, however, during this summer appears to have been phenomenal. "The pilchards have brought the other fish in with them," states the *Cornwall Gazette*, "and our markets are supplied with the greatest abundance and variety—cod, ling, hake, pollock, whiting, mackerel, mullet, bass, soles, turbot, etc.—all at very low prices, and pilchards almost for nothing."[2] Five years later, however, the fishing showed a very different aspect. "The season is now almost come," states the *Cornwall Gazette*, 18 July, 1807, "when it was usual to commence our great pilchard fishery;

[1] Courtenay, Royal Cornwall Polytechnic Society, Report 1838.
[2] *Cornwall Gazette*, 14 August, 1802.

but for the present season, scarcely a single pilchard has appeared. This, however, is of less consequence as the want of a market for the fish last year, and the still more discouraging prospects of the present, have extinguished all hope and expectation from this once fruitful source of our prosperity. Ten or a dozen seines will, we are informed, be the outside of what will be put to sea this year, and those to provide only for our own markets, and the trivial demands of the West Indies. The mackerel fishery of the present year also, as in the last, has been most unprofitable. In some seasons, these fish have confined their visits almost entirely to the coasts of Cornwall and Devon. But of late, while very few indeed have been caught here, we find they abound in vast shoals on the coast of Norfolk!"

As thus shown, in addition to the vagaries of the fish themselves, the renewal of war, after the short peace of 1802, had again presented the industry with the problem of finding markets. The demand for pilchards, it is true, remained unabated. In 1811, a cargo which had been sent out from Cornwall under licence was seized by the French, and through them sold to the Italians at the enormous price of £9 per hogshead.[1] Two years later, another cargo which reached Leghorn in safety, brought a like price to the enterprising Cornish merchants.[2] The outlet for pilchards, nevertheless,

[1] *West Briton*, 23 July, 1812.
[2] J. C. Bellamy, *Guide to the Fishmarket* (1843), 80.

was very much restricted, and during this time immense quantities were taken for their oil only, the fish, after pressing, being sold for manure. An attempt, indeed, was made to find a new vent for pilchards in the West Indies, for which market they were treated by pickling. Owing, however, to lack of knowledge, or care, in curing them, the fish got into disrepute, and the trade languished.[1] With the return of peace, and the gradual settlement of Europe after the Napoleonic wars, the exports resumed their accustomed channel and the fisheries benefited accordingly. In 1814 and 1815, the quantities taken were small, but the ports being now open, the fish brought high prices, rising in the latter year to one hundred and eight shillings per hogshead.[2] This was, of course, a "peak" year, and from that time onwards until 1837, prices fluctuated within the more sober limits of thirty shillings to eighty shillings per hogshead.

Nevertheless, a remarkable stimulus had been given to the industry by the return of normal trade. During the year 1827, the total number of seines in Cornwall, ashore and afloat, was three hundred and sixteen. Persons employed about the seines at sea numbered two thousand six hundred; those

[1] J. S. Courtenay, Royal Cornwall Polytechnic Society, Report 1838, 119-20.

[2] This was exclusive of the oil which varied from two to as much as seven gallons per hogshead of fish. In addition, the Government bounty of 8s. 6d. per hogshead continued, until 1829, to be paid on all pilchards exported to foreign markets. See Cornwall Polytechnic Society, Reports 1835, 1838.

THE FISHERMAN'S TRADE 169

directly engaged in the pilchard fishery on shore six thousand three hundred. In addition to the seines, there were more than three hundred and fifty drift boats, employing one thousand six hundred men. Altogether the full complement of persons employed in connection with these two main branches of the Cornish fishing industry numbered ten thousand five hundred; whilst the capital invested in the boats, nets, cellars, and other establishments on shore was close on £440,000. In the year 1830, the total quantity of pilchards sent to the Mediterranean ports from St. Ives alone amounted to some six thousand four hundred hogsheads; whilst during the years 1829-38 St. Ives supplied the Italian markets with an average of nearly nine thousand hogsheads annually.[2] In the season of 1832, a seine owner at Newlyn is said to have cleared £1,300 as the result of the enormous catches being taken at that time in Mounts Bay,[3] whilst on a yet more memorable occasion, in November 1834, no less than ten thousand hogsheads or thirty millions of fish were enclosed by the seines at St. Ives within an hour![4]

[1] Yarrell, *British Fishes*. Quoted by J. C. Bellamy, *Guide to Fishmarket*. The number of men and boats engaged in the fishery was subject to considerable fluctuation. In 1877, the total number of seines in Cornwall was 390, employing 1,024 men at sea. Drift boats in this year numbered 538, with 2,241 men afloat. Cf. Royal Cornwall Polytechnic Society, Report 1878, 94 and 98.

[2] *Western Morning News*, 21 September, 1921.

[3] *Western Antiquary* (1883), III, 77.

[4] J. Couch, Royal Cornwall Polytechnic Society, Report 1835, 83 and 98.

IV

Prior to the middle of the eighteenth century, the season for pilchards frequently extended from July till November or December, sometimes even into January or February. During the last century, however, the season generally commenced about the beginning of August, and lasted until the end of October, or, as the old people used to say:

> When the corn is in the shock
> Then the fish are on the rock.

As the time for their arrival drew near, a close watch was kept for the pilchards from the shore, and any indication of their approach was triumphantly hailed:

> See where the bird of force
> The quick-eyed gannet marks the pilchard's course,
> Darts with the lightning's flight amid the shoal
> And fills with rapturous hope the fisher's soul.
> Auspicious bird!
> Welcome, thrice welcome to our southern shore!
> At thy approach the seiner plies his oar,
> At thy approach the Huer, watchful still,
> Ascends with anxious step the prospect hill
> And if his eye discern the scaly host
> Waves the known signal and informs the coast.
> Then what a scene ensues! the teeming bay
> In long discoloured columns marks the prey,
> Thousands and tens of thousands, millions pour,
> And "Hevva, Hevva" rings along the shore.[1]

---

[1] *Cornwall Gazette*, 24 July, 1802.

At St. Ives, the launching of the great fleet of seine-boats, which during the off-season were drawn up on the grassy banks adjoining Porthminster beach, was a joyous occasion for all the children of the town. Crowding into the boats as they were dragged down across the sand into the sea, the children would sing:

> A laky (leaky) ship with her anchor down!
> Her anchor down, her anchor down!
> A laky ship with her anchor down,
> Hurrah, my boys, hurrah!
>
> We're loaded with sugar and rum, my boys!
> And rum, my boys, and rum, my boys!
> We're loaded with sugar and rum, my boys,
> Hurrah, my boys, hurrah!

Rocking the boats from side to side as they sang, the fleet, with its crew of happy youngsters, was launched into the blue waters of St. Ives Bay, and was then rowed round to the harbour to be fitted up with the nets, ropes, and other tackle required for the forthcoming season.

The unit known to the fishermen by the comprehensive term, a "seine," comprised three boats and two nets. The largest of the boats was a kind of galley, about forty feet long and twelve wide, combining burden with swiftness. It was equipped with a capstan and a space, called the net room, in which the gear was stored. Whilst lying off-shore, awaiting the arrival of the fish, a canopy or "tilt" was commonly erected in the bow, under which the crew were able to shelter in bad weather, and where they did their cooking. This boat, known as the *seine-boat*, was manned by six rowers and a steersman with, frequently, an eighth man to lend further assistance when the time came to "shoot," or pay out, the great net which it carried. The second boat, somewhat smaller, but manned by a like number of men, was called in St. Ives, the *tow-boat*, and in other places, the *follower*, from its always taking up a post in the rear of the *seine-boat*. The *tow-boat* carried a smaller net called the *tuck-seine*. The third boat, which was the smallest of all, was called, in St. Ives, the *follower*, and elsewhere, the *lurker* or *cock-boat*. It generally carried the master seiner and one or two lusty men.[1]

From the beginning of the season onwards, the seines were rowed out early in the morning, and remained throughout the day at anchor in their various stations, each one anxiously awaiting the signal from the huers who kept their watch on the cliff-top above. Owing to the seiners' dependence on wind and tide, and the necessity of speedy and well-ordered action, when once the school or schools of pilchards arrived, the coast line within the waters of the sandy bays was mapped out into clearly defined "stems" or stations, which were assigned to the various companies of seine owners at the beginning of each season by drawing lots. In St. Ives Bay, the fishing stems lying between Hayle Bar and the Island were known respectively

[1] *Cornwall Gazette*, 24 July, 1802.

as Carrack Gladden, the Leigh, the Pull, Porthminster, Pednolver, and Carrick Leggoe or Carn Crowse. Each of these was defined by means of two poles erected on the shore, one some distance behind the other, and the fishermen clearly understood that they must not trespass over the imaginary line which lay between these poles and extended indefinitely out to sea. Considering the great sums of money which were at stake, and the speed with which the schools of pilchards were capable of moving along the coast, some such arrangement was clearly needed, in order to prevent the violent conflicts which must undoubtedly have arisen had all the companies been free to make a rush for the most favourable position at the same time.

At length, perhaps, on some hot sleepy August afternoon, the huers would suddenly be startled into activity by the sight of certain reddish-brown patches of colour moving rapidly along beside the shore, close under the surface of the sea. "At one moment," writes Mr. Harris Stone, "the mass or school of pilchards—for such it is—may be a quarter of a mile in length, and even as you look it elongates and shoots out into half a mile, only to thicken up a few minutes later into a regular ball, more or less spherical. Immediately the fish are sighted the huer's trumpet blares forth, and the cry of 'hevva! hevva!' (Cornish *hesva*, a school of fish) goes up, and is quickly spread through the neighbouring town. Out from the streets and houses pours forth the whole population, for the arrival of the pilchards concerns all, the women and children, not less than the men. Meantime the huer, standing silhouetted on top of the hedge before his hut, is signalling frantically, with a 'bush' in each hand, to the boats which are awaiting his orders no less eagerly below. First he waves his two clubs to the eastward, and the men strain at the oars in an answer to his commands, then, with his whole body rapidly bending up and down, he directs the boats to take their course straight out to sea. At length, the psychological moment arrives, and the huer, dropping his bushes for a moment, yells through the long speaking trumpet to the men to shoot the seine." [1]

The seine-net itself was a formidable affair, being more than a quarter of a mile long, and about seventy feet wide or deep. Cork floats were attached to it at regular intervals along one edge and lead sinkers on the other. Altogether, the net with its floats, sinkers, and ropes weighed close on three tons. On the orders coming to shoot the seine, the fishermen would start to pay out the net, whilst the rowers at the same time pulled the boat through a large semicircle. With such vigour and alacrity was this work carried out that it was by no means uncommon for the whole of the net, with its rope, corks, and lead, to be thrown into the sea in less than five minutes.[2] Provided the bottom edge of the seine was touching the ground, and the top was

[1] *England's Riviera*, 43 et seq.
[2] J. Couch, Royal Cornwall Polytechnic Society, Report 1835, 74.

floating properly on the surface of the water, the fish had but little chance of escaping, but as it was difficult to bring the two ends of the great seine-net together all the way to the bottom, the smaller "stop-net," manipulated by the tow-boat, was paid out across the opening. Meantime the "follower" had also arrived at the starting point and set about joining up the seine- and the stop-nets, the crew at the same time beating the water with their oars in order to frighten the fish back. In this way, provided that everything went well, the fish were at length enclosed by a wall of net from which escape was impossible. By means of the many capstans dotted along the shore, the seine was then drawn into shallow water. Great care and judgment had to be exercised in this, for two or three days, or even as much as a week might elapse (if the catch was heavy) before the nets could be emptied of their haul. It was essential, therefore, that the water should be shallow enough to permit of the clearing process, and yet deep enough at all states of the tide to keep the fish alive until they could be landed.[1]

The net, therefore, having been manœuvred into position, and the weather and tides proving suitable, the work of "tucking" began. This consisted of lowering into the seine-net a small "tuck-net," one side of which was attached to the attendant boats. The tuck-net had long ropes by which it was raised to the surface of the water

[1] Mr. William Paynter, *Old St. Ives*, 39.

when full. "At the moment when the tuck-seine produces its burthen above water," states an old writer, "the sight, if the sun shines out, is beautiful beyond all description. Ten thousand lively little creatures, jumping and springing together, reflect from their burnished scales of blue and silver such a blaze of light and beauty as cannot be conceived by those who have never beheld it."[1] Meantime, the men, working with baskets, locally known as "whiskets," scooped up the fish from the tuck-net into their boats, till they were standing waist high in pilchards. As each of these attendant boats or "dippers" was filled, it was pulled for the shore, from whence its contents were removed by the "blowsers" or carriers to the innumerable cellars with which the fishing towns were furnished.

In places where approach to the cellars was impracticable for carts, "gurries" or boxes with four pole-handles were used, each gurry containing about a thousand pilchards. Gurry-watchers, armed with sticks, were frequently appointed to accompany these, in order to prevent people from stealing or "kaybing" the fish.[2] The story is told how on one occasion, Mr. B——, a leading seine owner, arrived on horseback at St. Ives in order to superintend the landing of a large school of pilchards which had just been enclosed on the beach. Riding down to the edge of the sea, he beckoned to a boy who was standing by, to come and hold his horse.

---

[1] *Cornwall Gazette*, 24 July, 1802.
[2] Mr. William Paynter, *Old St. Ives*, 39–40.

With "Bushes"

Comley, St. Ives

(See page 174)   With Trumpet

A Huer Signalling

"What 'll 'ee give me?" inquired the youth, with Cornish shrewdness.

"Give you? Oh, I'll give you sixpence."

"Shaen't do et," was the blunt reply. "Why I can get more 'en that kayben old B—'s pilchers."

Arrived at the cellars, the blowsers would find the women and children already waiting. Each gurry, as it came, was tipped out on to the ground, and the fish were seized upon by the children and handed to the women who laid them in layers along the cellar wall, with their heads pointing outwards. As each row of pilchards was completed, it was covered with a layer of salt, and on to this another layer of pilchards was laid, and so the pile went on increasing, until it was as high as the women could conveniently reach. This process, known as "bulking," often went on far into the night, and when the catch was a big one was continued for many nights in succession, the women and children coming from all the surrounding countryside in order to assist in the work which had to be done at high pressure. "During these strenuous nights," as Mr. W. Paynter has said, "the cellars presented scenes of extraordinary interest and activity. The dark background with its heavy shadows relieved at intervals by flickering candles, the burly porters dumping the fish on the ground, the women piling them up hour after hour, the attendant children with their 'whiskets' of salt and fish, and the 'bulks' themselves gleaming pink and pearly-grey, formed a picture likely to remain long in the memory of those privileged to have seen it." [1]

After remaining in bulk for some weeks, the fish were removed and placed in barrels in which they were pressed by means of heavy stones, in order to extract the residue of the oil which they contained. In earlier times, this oil was largely used for lighting purposes, a fact which explains the old saying: "Meat, money, and light, all in one night." Pilchard oil was also regarded by many Cornish people as a sovereign remedy for festering cuts and wounds. The squeaking noise made by the bursting of the air bladders whilst the fish were being pressed was called "crying for more," and was regarded as an omen that further catches of pilchards would soon be brought in to keep the others company. It was likewise said that the advent of a good haul of fish was presaged by a commotion among the "bullies" or pressing-stones, which between seasons were kept in the cellars, above which the fishermen lived.

At length when all the fish had been saved, the town crier in his "high-pole" (top) hat was sent round the streets and alleys in order to proclaim to all those who had been employed in connection with the various seines [2]—the "Amity," the "Success," the "Unity," the "Fisherman's Friend," the "Friend's Endeavour," or whatever the name of the company might be—that they were to

[1] Mr. William Paynter, *Old St. Ives*, 40.
[2] Mr. William Paynter, *Old St. Ives*, 41.

assemble at one or other of the inns in the town in order to be paid. In most cases, the seiners received a cheque for their share of the fish, and this they forthwith proceeded to divide amongst themselves. The writer has been told that in the old days at Sennen Cove it was usual for this cheque to be paid to the landlord of the one and only inn. The latter would then take it to Bolitho's bank in Penzance, and there exchange it for its equivalent value in sovereigns, half-sovereigns, and a good assortment of silver. On his return, all hands who were entitled to a share would assemble round a table at the inn. In addition to the active partners in the seine, there were generally five or six sleeping partners, as on the death of a married man, his share was continued to his widow for life or to his children until they were old enough to look after themselves. The pile of gold being placed in the middle of the table, the landlord would look round and say, "Well, boys, how much do 'ee think it'll go?" One of the men might perhaps suggest £5 or possibly £8, on which the landlord would place that amount in front of each. If any gold remained over, another guess would be made, and another share-out took place. The same process was then applied to the silver. If at the end a little odd money still remained, it was spent on drinks all round, whilst the few odd coppers were set aside for "niceys" (sweets) for the children.[1]

The method still employed in Sennen for dividing

[1] Per Mr. J. C. Hoare.

the catches of mullet which are sometimes taken there in considerable quantities, is no less interesting, and is probably still older in its origin. On being brought ashore, the fish is thrown on to the ground in piles, each pile being as nearly equal as the men can conveniently make it. Generally there are two piles to each man. When all the fish has been divided thus, one of the men goes round with a basket, and into it the others throw some little personal belonging, such as a knife, a tobacco box or the like. These are then thrown out at random on to the piles of fish, by which means each man is able to identify his share and feels, moreover, that he has received it by a fair and impartial allotment.[1]

In the case of the pilchard seines, the owners, after the men had received their shares, would sometimes contribute towards the cost of a supper for the women whom they had employed during the season. These "cellar-feasts," as they were called, were usually held in some sail-loft which had been fitted up for the occasion, and to them each woman was generally allowed to invite a friend. "Some pretty come out they was too!" an old St. Ives fisherman once remarked to the writer. "Every woman used to turn up in a clean sogget (apron), and after the supper there would be singing, dancing, and fiddling, going on till eleven o'clock at night sometimes. Plenty of fun all round, but little or no drinking."[2]

[1] Per Mr. Manning-Sanders.   [2] Per Mr. Edward Basset.

(*See pages* 152 *and* 176)   A SEINE OF PILCHARDS   *Comley, St. Ives*

V

The pilchard fishery was followed by that of the herring which were, as indeed they still are, taken with drift nets, along the north coast, up to Christmas. January and February were, generally speaking, poor months for the fishermen, but from March to the end of April, or sometimes later, the mackerel fishery was in full swing. With the disappearance of these fish from the home waters, it was customary for the fast-sailing, lugger-rigged fleets of Porthleven, Newlyn, Mousehole, and St. Ives to fit out for the North Sea herring fishery which was conducted principally from the ports of Whitby, Sunderland, Hartlepool, and Scarborough. Many of the Cornish boats, however, from as early as the seventeenth century onwards, were wont to show still greater enterprise, following the herring round the north of Scotland to the Isle of Man, and thence to the coast of Ireland.[1] Much of the Cornish fisherman's prosperity formerly depended on the success or otherwise of this fishery, which occupied two or three months of the year, and carried the men such great distances from home. Their enterprise, however, was not always crowned with the success which it deserved. On 2 August, 1839, we learn from the columns of the *West Briton* that the greater part of the St. Ives and Mounts

[1] Hobson Matthews, *History of St. Ives*, 339.

Bay boats had returned home from the herring fishery in Ireland, where the season had proved a complete failure. Not only was the number of fish taken very small but, owing to a combination among the buyers, the prices were so low as scarcely to recoup the fishermen for their outlay. "This," states the writer, "represents a great loss to Cornwall, as not less than two hundred and fifty boats from St. Ives and Mount's Bay were engaged in the Irish fishery this season."

During the summer of the same year, however, the pilchard fishery proved more successful, the fresh fish selling in the country districts at one shilling and eightpence per hundred and twenty, and those cured for exportation bringing fifty-two shillings per hogshead at the Mediterranean ports.[1] Throughout the ensuing decades of the nineteenth century, seasons of scarcity continued to alternate with others in which the markets were well-nigh glutted with the huge catches of fish. In the year 1847, the exports of pilchards from Cornwall amounted to 40,883 hogsheads or 122,000,000 fish, whilst the greatest recorded number ever taken in one seine was that of 5,600 hogsheads or 16,500,000 fish, at St. Ives in 1868.[2] After such catches, thirty or forty vessels might be seen at one time in the harbour at St. Ives, waiting to carry the fish away to Italy.[3]

It is sad, indeed, to have to relate that the whole

---

[1] *West Briton*, 4 October, 1839.
[2] *Victoria History of Cornwall*, 584. [3] Per Mr. Edward Basset.

of the inshore seine fishery, and the stirring life which went with it, has now become part and parcel of the bygone days, and the very memory of it is becoming lost with the death of the older generation. For some years before the end came, a great change had taken place in the method of dealing with the fish. Owing to the invention of curing in tanks, the process of laying the pilchards in bulk was entirely dispensed with, and as a result many hundreds of men, women, and children became robbed of their former means of support. The new process is said to have been introduced first at Mevagissey, and it is certainly a curious fact that not only did the pilchards shortly afterwards begin to desert that bay, but since the introduction of tanks has become general in all the fishing ports, the vast shoals of pilchards which formerly darkened the waters of the Cornish coast have no longer been seen. The year 1907 witnessed practically the last of the really big catches to be taken by the seining method, some eight thousand hogsheads or roughly twenty-four millions of fish having been netted that year in St. Ives Bay.[1] Since that time, the industry has steadily and persistently declined, and though a few seines are still kept in readiness at Coverack, and at one or two other coves along the south coast, this branch of the fishing industry may be said, for the time being at any rate, to be extinct.

Among the older generation of fishermen, there

[1] See *Western Morning News*, 21 September, 1921.

are still not a few who regard this fact as being a direct judgment of Heaven on the infamous invention of curing in tanks. Others, seeking a more rational explanation, ascribe it to the absence of the red water which formerly flowed into the sea from the surrounding mines, and which, so far from polluting the fishing grounds, is claimed to have served a useful purpose by thickening the waters of the bays in a manner which attracted the shoals of pilchards to lie therein. A more likely explanation, however, seems to lie in the vast increase of deep-sea trawling, in the Channel and elsewhere, which, by breaking up the shoals, and by destroying huge quantities of the immature fish, is everywhere robbing the inshore fisherman of his livelihood by cutting off his supplies at the source. Though this view is still questioned in some degree by the "experts," it is held by every practical Cornish fisherman with whom the writer has spoken, and it is certainly a striking fact that during the war, when trawling was largely in abeyance, mackerel, herring, and other fish were more plentiful in the inshore waters than they had been for many years previously.

Though the seining is now defunct, pilchards still represent an important section of the west-country share-fishing industry, and, as recently as the summer of 1929, phenomenal catches of these fish were landed at the Cornish ports. They are now taken, however, only at considerable distances from land, and are caught, like the mackerel and herring, in drift-nets. The latter resemble the seine-nets in so far as they have corks all along one edge, but no leads are attached to the other, since they are intended only for fishing in deep water where they do not reach the bottom. One end of the drift-net is fastened to the boat, and the other is carried out by the strong-flowing tide. Frequently twenty or more nets are fastened one on to the other, so that the whole combination is generally a mile or more in length, and stands in the water like a wall. As the fish come up with the tide, their heads become entangled in the meshes of the nets, from which they are not easily able to withdraw on account of their gills which open and operate like barbs.

The "shooting" of a long train of nets, and the thought of how much depends on the fortune which may attend them when once they have passed far out into the dark surrounding waters, is an occasion the significance of which is far from being lost upon minds so deeply imbued with religious feeling as those of the Cornish fishermen. To a visitor out with them in their boats, it is a moving experience to hear the murmured utterance of the prayer: "Lord, spare our labour, and send them in with a blessing. Amen"—with which words many crews are (or were, formerly) in the habit of consigning the first of their drift-nets to the deep. Those who know the Cornish fishermen, moreover, will hardly be surprised to learn that other practices of a yet older origin still survive among them, and that, in some cases, there lies embedded in the first of the cork floats, as it goes drifting out upon the tide, a silver coin,[1] placed there to-day, no doubt, more in jest than in earnest, and yet unconsciously fulfilling the custom instituted by their far-off ancestors who thus sought to propitiate the Spirit of the sea. Going below afterwards into their tiny, stuffy cabins, reeking with the smell of fish and strong tobacco, it was not unusual to see one of the older men turning to the pages of his Bible, whilst the good old Methodist hymns, which cheered their forefathers under like conditions, are still often raised by the fishermen of to-day, when riding beneath the stars on the dark rolling waters of the Atlantic.

After some hours of waiting thus, the time at length comes for the nets to be drawn in again on board, and this used to be the signal among the mackerel drivers for the calling of their ancient chant:

Brî'el, mâta, treja, peswara, pempes, wethes! "A mackerel, a fellow, a third, a fourth, a fifth, a sixth!" of which each man cried a word in turn as the first netted fish appeared, "a formula," as Mr. Nance has observed, "closely matched by fishermen in Scotland, and on the south and east coasts of England,"[2]—but of special interest in this case as being preserved in the ancient Celtic language of the Duchy.

[1] Per Mr. George Dunn, St. Ives.
[2] *Folklore Recorded in the Cornish Language*, 8–9.

VI

Until recent times, the drifting for mackerel continued to form one of the most important branches of the Cornish fishing industry, although it was principally confined to the boats of Mounts Bay and St. Ives. There were formerly two mackerel fisheries in the year, the one commencing in March and closing about the end of May, and the other extending from September to December. The fish taken in the spring were mostly consumed fresh; those caught in the autumn, being esteemed of better quality, were salted in in great numbers by the inhabitants of the county, for winter use. In the spring of 1838, over one hundred and twenty boats were engaged in this fishery at Newlyn, Mousehole, and Porthleven.[1] At this time, and, indeed, for many years later, the fish was principally marketed by the wives of the fishermen who hawked their husbands' catches through the adjoining towns and villages. One of the most pleasing and familiar sights of Penzance in those days was that of the Newlyn fishwives, who in their scarlet cloaks and large black beaver hats, might be seen daily in the streets. The fish itself was carried in "cowals" or specially-shaped baskets, which were supported on the women's

[1] Royal Cornwall Polytechnic Society, Report 1838, 130-1.

backs by a broad band which passed around their hats. With their fine symmetry, healthy complexions, curling ringlets, and blue eyes, they must indeed have presented a striking contrast to their sisters of the trade in London, and more than one traveller seems to have lost his heart to the beautiful fishwives of this town.[1]

With the opening of the Cornwall railway in 1859, changes of a far-reaching character took place. As a result of the direct communication now established with the metropolis, a new and important market was developed for the Cornish spring mackerel. Newlyn became the local depot for this trade, and thither was brought the whole of the catches of the Mounts Bay fleet. The fish train for London left at 2 p.m., and to get the catches home and landed in time for this, was the supreme effort of the day. To meet this necessity a new class of boat was built, designed especially for speed. By 1884, the number of mackerel drivers belonging to the county had increased to nearly four hundred, employing two thousand seven hundred men, the cost of the newer type of boat, with its full complement of nets and tackle, being approximately £600.[2]

Up to the time when Newlyn harbour was built, the Newlyn fleet had permanent moorings off the shore. At these moorings, each vessel kept a four-oared boat at anchor, by means of which the

[1] Cf. G. A. Cooke, *Topographical Description of Cornwall* (1830).
[2] Royal Institution of Cornwall, March 1884, Journal VIII, 12.

Gibson, Penzance

(See page 188) AN OLD FISH "JOUSTER"

THE FISHERMAN'S TRADE

crew, with their catches, were able to land on their return from the fishing grounds. It was a fine sight to see the great fleet of mackerel drivers riding off the shore, or the same number of small boats waiting at the moorings when the large ones were at sea. The Mousehole mackerel drivers differed from those of Newlyn in using a three-oared jollyboat to bring their fish ashore. Each of these was in the charge of a boy, from ten to fourteen years of age, who was engaged by the fishing lugger to whom the boat belonged at a wage of one shilling and sixpence a week. This "captain" of the jollyboat was known as a "yawler," a term peculiar to Mousehole where alone he was employed.

The yawler's duties, as described by Mr. William Pezzack, to whom the writer is indebted for the following information, were clearly defined. Whilst the season lasted, he was the absolute slave of the lugger by which he was employed. Early in the morning, often at daybreak, he would shoulder the two long oars required by the crew for pulling ashore and his own short "paddle" with which he himself sculled the jollyboat. Thus equipped, he would wend his way to the harbour, where he would find some fifty other yawlers, all busily engaged, if the tide were low, in helping each other to get afloat. As soon as the fleet was sighted in the offing, the flock of small craft would scull away to the best position for bearing down before the wind to "take" the lugger to which each one belonged. This "taking" was the great event of the yawler's day. As each lugger neared the coast her yawler would drop out of the waiting flock, and get right ahead of his boat, as it bore down upon him under full sail. The faster she was going, the greater his joy. With the jollyboat pointing the same way as the big boat, the yawler would wait with the coiled painter in his hand, ready for the critical moment when, with the foam piled up at her bows, the lugger rushed by. As she did so, the painter was nimbly thrown to those on board, and the yawler would crouch low in expectation of the jerk with which, as the rope became taut, his jollyboat sat up almost on end, with the water boiling up behind the stern as if intent on swamping her. "To be towed to Newlyn market in this style," writes Mr. Pezzack, "was a supreme joy. To miss this feat, was a disgrace too deep to be contemplated—and in practice it very rarely occurred, owing to the skill and judgment in manœuvring their craft which the boys attained."

If there was not enough fish to be worth taking to Newlyn, the yawler had only to come alongside when the big boat anchored, in order to take the crew ashore. At other times, when the fleet of luggers was becalmed, the yawlers would often scull out two or three miles to meet them and take off the fish, which would then be rowed in to Newlyn by one or two of the younger members of the lugger's crew.

Very often, the yawler had a strenuous time

getting out, against wind and tide, to the proper position where he could be taken up by the incoming fleet. The jollyboats were always equipped with a kedge rope with a stone attached to one end. When so much exhausted that they could scull no more, the boys would drop anchor for a time, and rest. Then, as they felt able to renew the struggle, they would take to their scull once more and so press on until they reached the desired position for being taken up. Often the fleet itself would be expected about breakfast or dinnertime, and the yawler, in consequence, knew the pangs both of hunger and thirst, as he waited long and patiently at his post. Great was his satisfaction, however, if he could manage to get on board his lugger when at length she arrived and regale himself with the warm black tea, bits of fish, and stale bread left over from the crew's own meal.

Whilst the fleet was at sea, the yawler was at liberty to amuse himself as best he liked. There was no prank with wind or waves that he would not try. Knowing, as he did, every trick and temper of his own jollyboat, he would manœuvre and propel her into nooks and crannies, round the rocks, and in and out of the breaking sea, rejoicing in the dangers which he evaded by his skill.

The yawlers were not all boys, however. A few of them were aged fishermen who, no longer having strength for the strenuous life at sea, had returned to their boyhood's job, and did it well. Some of these old men still continued to wear the tall "stove-pipe" hats of their earlier days. The sight of these, tilted on the backs of their owners' venerable heads, caused no small amusement to the boys, as they watched them swaying from side to side in their rolling, pitching boats. But although they sometimes laughed at their old-fashioned ways and notions, the boys respected them too, for when they could be got to talk, these weather-beaten old men would tell of the days long past, of their hairbreadth escapes in open boats, of being hunted by the press-gang, of smuggling and wrecking, and other incidents of their exciting and venturous youth.[1]

The employment of the yawler, as Mr. Pezzack has said, produced a class of men supremely expert in the management of small craft, and consequently a type of sailor particularly suited for the handling of yachts, a profession in which many of them were subsequently engaged. With the completion of the harbour at Newlyn, however, the day of the yawler came to an end, since the fishing fleet, by being able to enter port and discharge its catches directly on to the quays, no longer required the assistance of the jollyboats. The construction of Newlyn harbour, moreover, was contemporaneous with the beginning of a rapid decline in the prosperity of the Mounts Bay mackerel fishery, a decline which has since resulted in the

[1] "The Yawlers of Mousehole," *Cornishman*, 31 October and 13 November, 1929.

disappearance of the whole of the famous fleet of drifters once owned by these ports.

The story of the collapse of this great branch of the Cornish fishing industry dates back in its origin to the time when the "up-country" trawlers first began to frequent the western waters. As long ago as 1843, the menace of this new type of fishing operation had been noticed by at least one keen observer. Writing in that year, Doctor Bellamy stated: "Fishing, taken generally, interferes in the slightest way with the habits of the creatures in question; but the employment of a trawl, during a long series of years, must assuredly act with the greatest prejudice towards them. Dragged along with force over considerable areas of marine bottom, it tears away, promiscuously, hosts of the inferior beings there resident, besides bringing destruction on multitudes of smaller fishes, the whole of which, be it observed, are the appointed diet of those edible species sought after as human food. It also disturbs and drags forth the masses of deposited ova of various species. An interference with the economical arrangement of Creation, of such magnitude, and of such long duration, will hereafter bring its fruits in a perceptible diminution of these articles of consumption for which we have so great necessity. The trawl is already fast bringing ruin on numbers of the poorer orders requiring the most considerable attention. The fishermen of Cawsand complain to me that their profits gradually lessen, and point to the reckless destruction of spawn and young fish by trawlers, as the great source of their misfortunes."[1]

Elsewhere in Cornwall it seems that the disastrous effects of trawl fishing were not fully appreciated until considerably later than this. Prior to the opening of the Cornwall railway, the number of trawlers, who at that date mostly hailed from Plymouth or Brixham, was small, and the time during which they continued their operations was limited by their having to run to Plymouth, sixty miles off, in order to reach the nearest market. They only, therefore, trawled by day, whilst the local mackerel drivers had the grounds to themselves at night, which was all that they desired.[2] Up to this time not only did mackerel abound in the home waters in such numbers that in some seasons a single boat might bring in more than four thousand of them as the result of one night's draught, but hook-and-line fish were equally plentiful all along the south coast. In March 1802, ling of the best quality were being taken in Mounts Bay at the rate of ten or eleven hundred a day by single boats,[3] whilst a few years later it is recorded that as many as forty thousand hake were landed at Newlyn and Penzance within the space of twelve hours.[4] In addition to these extraordinary catches, the choicer grades of fish were

[1] *Guide to the Fishmarket*, 52, 140.
[2] *Cornish Telegraph*, 2 April, 1878.
[3] *Cornwall Gazette*, 13 and 27 March, 1802.
[4] J. C. Bellamy, *Guide to the Fishmarket*, 54.

procurable in the local markets throughout the year.

With the coming of the railway, however, the facilities for speedy communication with London which had so much benefited the local mackerel drivers, also resulted in a vast increase in the number of visiting trawlers. When in the year 1878 the Government at length decided to hold an inquiry, the latter were said to number more than a hundred, many of them being east-country boats. These vessels now trawled over the best mackerel driving grounds, day and night, from February to April, frequently fouling and cutting the nets of the local drifters. Feelings between the two opposing interests ran very high, and many of the witnesses who were called stated that the trawlers not infrequently made zigzag tracks across the drift-nets for the express purpose of destroying them, hoping, by such tactics, eventually to oust the local men from the field.[1]

In addition to the economic factor, religious differences added increased rancour to the dispute. True to their own lights in refusing to go to sea on Sunday themselves, the Newlyn men felt it to be more than they could stand that their rivals, scouting such sentiments, should be allowed to land their ill-gotten catches within their own harbour. At length, in May 1896, the storm which had so long been impending, broke. Seeing the east-country men returning one Monday morning

[1] *Cornish Telegraph*, 2 April, 1878.

from the fishing grounds, the Newlyn men put out to meet them in their boats, with the intention of throwing the fish overboard. Realizing this, the trawlers turned away and put into Penzance. Back went the Newlyn men to their port, and immediately started breaking up everything they could lay hands on with which to make weapons for the coming affray. Armed in this manner, they set off for Penzance and here, at the eastern end of the promenade, they met their rivals, and a hand-to-hand fight ensued. In the meantime, however, soldiers had been telegraphed for from Plymouth, and on their arrival very soon succeeded in quelling the riot.[1]

Though peace was restored, the causes which had given rise to the disturbance still remained. There is, indeed, something rather pathetic about this last ineffectual outburst on the part of those who were engaged in an old traditional industry. Faced as the hand-loom weavers had once been, with economic changes which were robbing them of their very means of livelihood, and understanding little of the underlying causes which made such changes inevitable, the Mounts Bay fishermen, in resorting to force, were but following out the blind instinct for self-preservation. Circumstances, however, were too powerful for them, and with the coming in later years, not only of increasing numbers of trawlers, but of the large steam drifters, who are able to use three miles of net to the local

[1] See *Western Morning News*, 13 January, 1930.

fisherman's one, besides being far less dependent upon weather, the fate of the Mounts Bay sailing fleet was sealed. For many years they struggled on against the ever-increasing odds; but now, at length, the time has come when they have been completely driven from their own ground. As a consequence, therefore, the fishermen of Newlyn, Mousehole, and Penzance may be seen to-day in the mackerel season eking out an existence by acting as porters and carriers to their rivals, who now land their catches on the quays from which, but a few years since, their own fleet so proudly sailed.

VII

It must not be assumed, of course, despite the loss of the inshore pilchard seining, and the rapid decline of the local mackerel drifting, that the Cornish fishing industry is a thing of the past. "There are still," wrote Mr. Howard Dunn in 1927, "about eleven or twelve hundred local fishermen, whose numbers are augmented, at various times, by approximately two thousand three hundred North Sea fishermen, and sometimes as many as a thousand Frenchmen or Bretons, the latter fishing the waters off the Cornish coast and taking their catches home to France. The fishermen, therefore, and the packers, curers, coopers, and box-makers, together with the capital invested in the boats, nets, gear, stores, smoke-houses (for kippering) and ice-works, still form no mean part of the county's stock-in-trade, whilst in recent years the annual value of the catches landed at the Cornish ports has approximated to £400,000."[1]

A quite considerable income is still derived, moreover, from other types of fishing than those already mentioned, the more important among these being the long-line, and the crab and lobster fisheries, both of which take place during the spring and summer. The results of all these classes of

[1] Cornwall "Education Week" Handbook (1927), 115.

THE FISHERMAN'S TRADE

fishing, however, are subject to great fluctuations, dependent, as they are, not only on the migrations of the fish themselves, but on the favourable or adverse conditions of the weather. In some seasons, one class of fish may be present in abundance, whilst in another it will be conspicuous by its almost complete absence. The year 1929, for instance, proved on the whole to be a very successful one for the Cornish fisherman. During the long-line season, great quantities of dog-fish were taken on the hook. This fish, which was formerly of no marketable value, has of late years become much sought after, being sold in the up-country markets under the name of "flake." [1] The pilchard season of the same year was likewise a success in the western waters, where some of the boats grossed about £600 down over a period of fourteen weeks. On the other hand, in the southeastern area, embracing Looe, Polperro, Mevagissey, and Fowey, this particular fishery was practically a failure. The herring season, which in that year commenced rather earlier than usual, gave every promise of success, a promise, however, which was, in a large measure, offset by the subsequent violence of the weather, which necessitated the restriction of operations in Port Isaac, Padstow, and Newquay, in all of which ports the men made very poor returns. Even in St. Ives, where, with few exceptions, the fleet did remarkably well in the matter of fish, there were more nets lost than

[1] *West Briton*, 2 January, 1930.

had ever been previously recorded in any season. Some boats lost anything up to a whole fleet of nets, a mile in length. As the boats only, and not the tackle, are insured by the society, such losses detracted very considerably from what might otherwise have been a highly successful season.[1] The great increase in the shoals of pilchards and herrings met with during this year, might reasonably have been supposed to augur well for the next, but yet in the summer of 1930 the pilchard season was described as an "utter failure," and the worst one on record for fifty years past. The long-line fishery was stated at the same time to have been equally unsuccessful, in some cases the men not grossing enough money to cover their out-of-pocket expenses. Yet in this very year, which proved so disastrous for other forms of fishing, the landings of the boats engaged in the crab fishery exceeded those of the corresponding seasons for ten years past.[2]

These facts, culled from the fishery officer's reports, show clearly enough the precarious and uncertain nature of the fisherman's livelihood. The effect of the unrestricted operations of the deep-sea trawlers is constantly being shown by the "patchy" nature of such shoals of fish as now find their way into the inshore waters. None know this better than the fishermen themselves, who realize that a successful season to-day is far

[1] *West Briton*, 2 January, 1930.
[2] *West Briton*, 18 December, 1930.

more a question of luck than ever it was in the past. The result is that, owing to the constant discouragements which the industry has received, the number of young men entering its ranks is small indeed, and year by year the number grows less. "Scarcity of men to fill the available boats is one of the most serious factors of the fisheries in various Cornish ports," wrote the local correspondent of the *Western Morning News* on 17 October, 1928. "In Mounts Bay, during the recent pilchard season, a few boats would have been unable to proceed to sea, but for the addition of visiting Newlyn and east coast fishermen to assist in working them. From the port of St. Ives owners of boats were yesterday visiting the various Mount's Bay ports in search of men to make up their crews, but were, in some cases, unsuccessful." During the spring and early summer of 1931, the long-line fishery was also severely handicapped by the difficulty of obtaining men. At one port in the south-eastern area, nearly fifty per cent of the fleet was laid up through failure to obtain crews to work the boats.[1] It is clear from this, that if the decline in the number of men continues at its present rate, the nation as a whole will shortly be deprived, not only of a source of its food supply, but of a fine race of seafarers which, until recently, has provided it with a valuable recruitment for the navy and the merchant service.

It is obvious, therefore, that the restoration of

[1] *West Briton*, 18 June, 1931.

the declining fortunes of the inshore fisheries of Cornwall, as elsewhere, is a matter of more than local concern. That this is realized to some extent is shown by the fact that the Government itself is now participating in the research which is being carried out with regard to the migrations of fish. Such a policy, it is hoped, may lead ere long to fruitful results, whilst international agreement with regard to trawling should prove of even greater value in restoring prosperity to the industry. It would seem, however, that something more, even than a partial return of fish to the coast, is necessary, if the fisheries of Cornwall are to be re-established upon an entirely satisfactory basis. The present methods of buying and distributing fish are both antiquated and wasteful. Whilst it is generally agreed by all parties that there exists, throughout the country, a large and unsatisfied demand for fish, yet when, as in the summer of 1929, unusually large quantities of pilchards made their appearance in the home waters, the fishermen were informed by the merchants that their requirements were satisfied, and that they could take no more fish from them, even if they were brought to land. That such a situation could ever arise, would seem due, in no small part, to the subsequent methods employed in distributing the fish. As things stand at present, the local buyers sell to commissioned agents at Billingsgate, who sell in turn to distributors, who sell to the retail traders, who sell to the public. Each buyer, of course, takes his profit from the next until, at length, the price which has been paid to the fisherman may have been multiplied ten times over before it is charged up to the consumer. To the unemployed population of our inland towns, there must, indeed, be a tragic irony in the constantly reiterated slogan: "Eat more Fish," when it is realized that the "rings" which have adopted this expensive method of gaining new customers are chiefly responsible in making the goods they advertise too dear for those same potential customers to buy.

For the fisherman, of course, the position is equally unsatisfactory although it must be admitted that he, to a certain extent, has himself to blame, having never given to the various attempts at co-operative selling the full measure of his support. Time and again co-operative marketing societies have been established at the Cornish ports. In some cases, these bodies have functioned successfully for three or four years, afterwards dwindling to nothing through the disloyalty of their members. Discussing the matter on a recent occasion with a *Western Morning News* reporter, a Porthleven fisherman remarked: "We had a co-operative marketing society here at one time, but it failed for the same reason as in other places. We were getting good prices for ourselves, but a private salesman came along and offered better. Some of our members took the short-sighted view and went over with him. This led to the break-up of the society. Personally, I think we should be doing better to-day if we had kept the society going. But that is the chief fault of Cornish fishermen, they are so jealous of each other that they will not work together and, unlike the farmers, we have no union to represent us. I am afraid the industry will be no better until the Cornish fishermen can be taught to realize that unity is strength." [1]

[1] *Western Morning News*, 13 February, 1931.

VIII

Whilst a consistent loyalty in supporting the co-operative marketing societies would undoubtedly help the fisherman to obtain better prices even under present conditions, it is clear that the industry itself must be subjected to a complete overhauling and reorganization if it is to survive in the new "big business" era of the twentieth century. As Mr. W. D. Jamieson recently pointed out in the *Daily Chronicle*, "there is little doubt that a large section of the Scottish fishery was suffering twenty years ago from conditions very similar to those under which the west country now labours. First, in the north, the trawlers killed the prosperous line fishing, then the beam trawl scooped in the white fish, and the outlook for the local fishermen appeared black indeed. Then, a day came when the first of the steam drifters arrived. To the sail-boat, of course, this meant strenuous competition, but the drifter was seen to be obviously the craft of the future and their number quickly multiplied. Every man who could afford it, built his own. In other cases, whole families combined together, sold their old craft, and invested all their savings in the new. In other cases again, the banker showed himself willing to lend his aid, and to-day many of the small ports in the north of Scotland, in which the outlook was once as dark as it still is in Cornwall, are equipped with fleets of thirty or forty drifters which drive a profitable trade. Where the boats are entirely financed by capitalists, as many of them are, the transition from being his own master to the status of a wage-earner must certainly have been a hard one for the share-fisherman, but it is in keeping with the natural trend of the times, and it is surely better than extinction? The question has often been asked, is there no available capital for such purposes in Cornwall and Devon? Are there no men of commerce who can see in this matter a sound investment? Cornwall, of course, is far from the great markets, and also from some of the newer fishing grounds, but mechanical devices in the steam-driven craft have eliminated distance. The Scottish fishermen now follow the herring far afield round the British Isles, while their womenfolk come as far west as St. Ives in order to do the work of kippering, which, surely, Cornish girls might learn to do as well? It is hard to see why things should remain as they now are, or why the Cornish fisherman should not follow where his Scottish brethren have so successfully led the way."

Such remarks, coming as they do from one who has witnessed changes of such a far-reaching importance in another great branch of the fishing industry of this country, would at any time have provided stimulating food for thought, but to-day their purport has taken on a new significance owing to the appearance of the modern Belgian motor trawler in the western waters. This has given an entirely new trend to the whole industry, and is at present causing embarrassment, not only to the Cornish fishermen, but even, in some degree, to their former vanquishers, the east-country men. It is only, indeed, within the last few years that this new phase of foreign competition has begun seriously to be felt. Prior to the war, the Belgians, so far from rivalling British fleets, were content, in many cases, to buy up out-worn Brixham smacks with which to conduct their own fisheries. Since that time, however, their whole outlook has changed. Assisted, *in part*, by governmental subsidies or cheap loans, the Belgian fishermen have condemned their old craft, and entered upon the construction of the finest type of sea-going vessel, equipped with the very latest form of motive power.[1] During the very time, in fact, when English fishermen, and in particular those of the west country, have been driven by force of circumstances to lay up their craft, their Belgian confrères have been forging ahead, and the sight of their boats is now a familiar one in almost every port along the south coast. Before the war, Brixham possessed about two hundred and fifty sailing craft—to-day the number is less than fifty, and these are rapidly being sold off for yachts and houseboats. As against this, we have the official figures of the Ostend fleet, which in 1920 consisted of ninety-

[1] See *Western Morning News*, 13 January, 1931.

five sailing smacks, thirty-three steam trawlers, and seven motor trawlers. Since that time Ostend has "scrapped" all its sailing craft, and now owns some thirty-five steam trawlers, and over two hundred and fifty motor trawlers.[1] Referring to a visit paid to this port at the beginning of 1931, an authority on Cornish fishing stated that he found there more than a dozen new motor vessels under course of construction, whilst the further orders, at that time received, were sufficient to keep the yards busy for another two years to come.

Such trawlers are stated to cost £6,000 apiece, and are fitted with Diesel engines and mechanical devices of the latest type. In competing with these vessels, the English steam-driven craft, costing more to build, and using a more expensive type of fuel, to say nothing of the greater number of hands which they require, seem likely to be relegated to an inferior position in the future.[2] There is, indeed, no little irony in the way in which history appears about to repeat itself. When the east-country boats came to Mounts Bay, they revolutionized the older industry which they found there, and the local fishermen, adhering too conservatively to their old ways, have in consequence been nearly wiped out. But, whilst Cornwall lost its mackerel fishery through the advent of the Lowestoft and Yarmouth drifters and trawlers, it now looks as if it may be the turn of the latter to give way to their

[1] Mr. W. J. Modley, *Western Morning News*, 10 June, 1931.
[2] *Western Morning News*, 17 January, 1931.

still more efficient Belgian competitors. It is, of course, too early to say yet what steps will be taken by the east-country owners to meet this new situation. But whatever the future may have in store for *them*, it clearly holds out little promise for the Cornish fisherman, equipped only with his tiny craft with which to face a competition which can cause something akin to dismay even among his erstwhile vanquishers.

For the local industry, perhaps one of the most disturbing factors in the present situation is the new type of trawl which the Belgian craft are said to be employing. The trawling operations of the east-country fleets have already proved sufficiently disastrous in destroying immature fish, and in breaking up the larger "schools" before they reach the inshore waters, but the new Belgian trawl-nets are alleged to be of smaller mesh than any which have previously been used by British craft. As a local fisherman recently declared: "Nothing can escape from these trawls. They are worse than fly-nets. They simply murder every immature fish that comes into them."[1] This, again, is clearly a matter which will have to be dealt with by international agreement, seeing that it is of vital concern, not only to British fishermen, but to all those who make use of the fishing grounds of the Channel and the North Sea. Meantime, intensive trawling is also prejudicing the long-line fishery, which was one of the last remaining assets of the

[1] *Western Morning News*, 16 May, 1931.

local industry, and which hitherto has partly compensated the Cornish fisherman for the loss of the mackerel drifting. To-day, however, owing to the danger of entanglement of his line of hooks with the trawl, and still more on account of the fact that the latter is sweeping bare the grounds where the boulter boats formerly went, the Cornish fisherman is being driven to seek more and more distant fields, and when at length he returns to port, it is only to find, in many cases, that his competitors with their fast-driven craft have already taken possession of the quays and landing places.[1] In some instances, the greater portion of the Belgian catches have not only been disposed of, but actually put on rail before the local men's fish can be sold, whilst harder still is the case where the Cornishman, on entering his own ports, is told by the buyers that the present demand is satisfied, and he sees the fish which he has toiled all night to get, being carted away into the countryside for manure.

Were the three-mile limit, which under modern conditions is clearly of little value, to be extended to twelve, as has been suggested, it might aid in ridding the present situation of some of its more grievous anomalies, and help to tide the local industry over a period in which the country at large is deciding whether it shall be reorganized or allowed to perish. For, as has already been pointed out, such reorganization necessitates, first and foremost, the capitalizing of the industry.

[1] *Western Morning News*, 23 April, 1931.

The western fishermen, whilst clearly recognizing the increased catching powers of their foreign competitors, claim that the new type of vessel which the situation demands is beyond their financial resources to supply. This being the case, the fleets must be modernized, either through the assistance of the financier or by co-operative effort, unless, of course, the work can be entirely effected through state subsidies or loans, which at the moment appears unlikely.

The problem, of course, presents other difficulties besides that of finding the necessary money for the building of new boats. Many of the present Cornish ports are clearly unsuited for the introduction of a larger type of craft, requiring sufficient depth of water for exit and ingress at all states of the tide. The changes which have been suggested would, therefore, undoubtedly mean the partial abandonment of such ports, in favour of others which are better endowed in this respect. Fortunately, Cornwall has no lack of deep-water harbours, especially along its southern shore, and the development in these of a new type of fishing should not present great difficulty.

Harder, no doubt, must be the task of convincing men so "set" in their ways as the share-fishermen of Cornwall that the time has come when they, like their northern brethren, must face the facts of the changing economic world in which they live, and subject themselves to a transition which cannot prove other than painful to those who have so long prided themselves on their independence and the personal ownership of their craft. Moreover, Cornish fishermen have never taken to deep-sea trawling, and although a few of them have done a little of this class of fishing, inshore: drifting, long-lining, and crabbing have always (with the addition of seining) been their chief vocations. Faced as they now are, however, with the entire loss of seining, together with a large part of their former drift fishing, and seeing, year by year, the better-equipped fleets of their foreign and east-country rivals scouring the seas from the Eddystone to Trevose, the time cannot be far distant when the realization will be borne in upon them that they *must* reorganize or perish.

Once these facts are recognized, the necessary change in attitude on the part of the men themselves may be rapid. For the fisherman comes of the same stock as the miner. Altering conditions in industry have long ago taught the latter how to adapt himself to new methods, and he is no longer suspicious of the changes which have added so largely to his material welfare. Nor need the older fishermen, who still cling to their former ways, despair of a livelihood. The crab and lobster fishery which now constitutes the most important branch of the industry in the smaller coves, does not stand in need of the same drastic reorganization, and may long continue to flourish on its present lines. But the fact remains that for the industry at large, changes of a radical nature will have to be made if it is ever to regain the status and prosperity which it once enjoyed. In fishing, as in all other forms of economic life, the day of the small unit is over and past. Deep-sea trawling has come to stay, and though the latter is likely to be increasingly regulated in the future by international agreement, it is in the development of this particular branch of fishing that the only hope of a returning prosperity for the sober hard-working seafarers of Cornwall appears to lie.

INDEX

Angel Hotel, 68
Arundell, family of, 83
Autobiography of a Cornish Smuggler, 5 note, 34

"Balking-house," 152
Baring-Gould, Rev. S., 97 note, 122, 123 note
Beach-combing, 111
Belgian motor trawlers, 207-10
Bellamy, J. C., 193
Bodmin gaol, 117
Bonham, Mrs., 115
Borlase, George, 24, 89, 93
Borlase, Dr. William, 159, 160 note
Bottrell, William, 30, 38
Brixham Trawlers, 194, 207
"Bushes," 152, 174

Camborne Miners, 104
Carew, Richard, 150-3, 156
Cecil, Sir Robert, 154
"Cellar-feasts," 180
"Cock-boat," 172
Connerton, Manor of, 79, 83
Constabulary force, report of, 107
Coode, Samuel, 84
Co-operative marketing, 203
Cornish, J. B., 35, 36, 70

Cornish jury, 26
Cornwall railway, 188, 194
Corpses, burial of, 97, 98
Couch, Jonathan, 160 note, 169 note, 174 note
Courtenay, J. S., 160 note, 161 note, 168 note
Courtney, M. A., 29, 93, 96
"Cousin Jack," 62
Crab fishery, 200, 212
"Cruel Coppinger," 28, 29
Curtis, John, 121
Czar of Russia, 126

Death ship, 30
Dog-fish, 199
Drift Fishing, 151, 165, 169 note, 185, 186, 195, 205, 208
Drift nets, 151, 185
Drinking, 62
Dunkirkers, 157-8
Dunn, Howard, 146, 198
Dunn, Mathias, 24

East-country fishermen, 195, 198, 201, 208
Ellenglaze, 80
Excisemen, 7, 17, 19 et seq., 23, 26, 37, 38, 46, 69, 92, 105, 110; Bribery of, 14, 23; Errors of, 10, 11

Falmouth Packets, 37
Fast-days, 149
Fish auctions, 142
Fisherman's prayer, 185
Fishermen, character of, 139, 141, 153, 159, 180, 184, 185, 186, 191, 195, 204, 211
Fishermen, shortage of, 201
Fishery officer, reports of, 199–200
Fishing: Capitalization of, 205 et seq., 211; Cawsand Bay, 147; Dangers of, 137 et seq.; Eighteenth Century, 159 et seq.; Elizabethan, 147 et seq.; Newlyn, 188, 190, 195; Newquay, 145, 162, 199; Penzance, 165, 194; Regulations of, 142, 147, 172; Seventeenth Century, 143, 150; Sixteenth Century, 151 et seq.; St. Ives, 143, 144, 153, 160 note, 169, 171, 172, 199; Thirteenth Century, 146
Fishing toasts, 163
Fish prices, 140, 161, 162, 165, 167–9, 182, 199, 202, 203
"Follower," 172, 175
Foxwell, Mr., 123
French Ships, 57, 58

Gaol fever, 19
George, Ann, 46
Giddy, Edward, 25, 27
Gilbert, Davies, 97
Godolphin, William, 82
Gold coinage, 111, 118
Great Work Mine, 88
Grenfell, Lewis 63

Hawker, Rev. R. S., 28
Hayle Railway, 14.
Heath, Robert, 86
Henderson, C. G., 80, 83, 84, 86, 97
Herring fishery, 137, 149, 150, 181, 199
"Hevva," 143, 170, 173
Huer, 145, 151, 165, 170, 173–4

"Informer," 63
Irish fishery, 150, 181
Irish wherries, 25
Italian merchants, 163–4
Italy, pilchards sent to, 163, 167, 182

Jamieson, W. D., 205
"Jollyboats," 189 et seq.

"Kaybing," 176–7
"Kiddleywinks," 9, 62
Killigrew, Lady, 86
Killigrew, Sir John, 85, 86
King's evidence, 47, 52
King of Portugal, 81
Kippering, 198, 206

Lee, George, 117
Lifeboats, 129, 131–3
Life-saving, 99, 119, 120, 123, 124, 127, 128 et seq.
Lizard lighthouse, 85, 86
Long-lining, 199, 205, 209, 212
"Lurker," 172

INDEX

Mackerel boats, 188
Mackerel chant, 186
Mackerel fishery, 167, 181, 187-8, 192 et seq.
Manby's mortar, 124
Matthew, Hobson, 150 note, 181 note
Methleigh, 80, 84, 97
Methodism, 5, 33, 186
Middlemen, 139 et seq., 202
Milaton, John, 82
Mounts Bay fleet, 181, 187, 197
Mylor, 11

Napoleonic Wars, 41, 44, 164, 165, 167, 168
Nance, R. Morton, 186
Nancekuke, 80
Net making, 146, 162
"Newcastle," 9
Newfoundland trade, 154-5
Newlyn fish-wives, 187-8
Newlyn riot, 195-6

"Old Dutchy," 71
Old, Stanley, 60, 65 note, 109, 111, 118
Ostend, 207, 208

Paynter, William, 175 note, 177
Peace of Amiens, 41, 165
Penrose, Edward, 84
Person, Francis, 81
Pezzack, William, 189, 190-2
Pilchards: Bounty on, 161, 168 note; Bulking of, 177; Curing in tanks, 183; For manure, 144, 165, 168; Oil from, 161, 168, 178; Pressing of, 178; Quantities of, 144, 161, 165, 169, 182, 183, 199, 202.
Pilotage, 129, 130
Pirates, 86, 156, 157, 158
Predannack, 80
Pressgang, 9, 192
Preventive Service, 48, 49
Prior of St. Nicholas, 79
Prussia Cove, 35, 36

Raleigh, Sir Walter, 154
Rawlings, William, 27 note
Right of Wreck, 79, 84
Roberts, Tobias, 123
Rocket Apparatus, 124 et seq.

St. Agnes' Lighthouse, 86, 113
St. Aubyn, Thomas, 82
St. Erth Bridge, 66
St. Ives diary, 128 et seq., 144
Salee rovers, 157-8
Salt for curing, 161-2, 177
"Salt Works," 146
Salvage, 129, 130
Scillonians, 21, 49, 86, 96, 97, 127
Scottish fisheries, 205-6
Seine-boats, 153, 171
Seine-nets, 174, 185
Seiners, payment of, 179-80
Seines, cost of, 162, 165
Seining, 143, 144, 151, 170 et seq.
Shairp, Alexander, 105
Share fishermen, 139-42, 165, 203
Shore, H. N., 50, 55

Shovel, Sir Cloudesley, 93 et seq.
Silver dollars, 112, 113
Skinner, Rev. J. S., 162
Smith, Rev. G. C., 113
Smugglers: Benallack, Peter, 55; Carter, Harry, 5; Daring of, 17 et seq., 42, 43, 53, 65; Generosity of, 60; Honesty of, 33, 34; "King of Prussia," 34 et seq.; Kinsman, Melchisideck, 8; "Lean Jack," 20; Mayor of Penzance, 23; Oats, 52; Pentreath, *alias* "Doga," 33; Permewan, 52; Plunkett, Patrick, 26; Pollard, Christopher, 44 et seq.; Royal Pardon for, 44; Trevaskis, 13 et seq.; Tricks of, 13, 19, 21, 22, 23, 39, 49, 51, 53, 56, 57, 59, 60, 63, 65, 66, 68; Violence of, 7, 8, 11, 17 et seq., 25, 45, 46.
Smuggling: by Tinners, 38; Cawsand Bay, 49, 50, 54; Channel Islands, 25; Decay of, 71; Definitions of, 6; Eighteenth century, 16 et seq.; Falmouth Packets, 37; Fowey, 7; Gorran, 67; Gunwalloe, 17; Gwithian, 65; Helston, 68; King Harry Passage, 43; Letters concerning, 24, 25; Mevagissey, 24, 59; Millbrook, 59; Mousehole, 20; Newquay, 23; Padstow, 22, 27, 60, 64; Penalties of, 55, 56; Penzance, 19, 20; Polperro, 42, 59; Porthoustock, 21; Portloe, 67; Prussia Cove, 33 et seq., 51; Report on in 1783, 16;

Roscoff, 5, 38, 50; St. Ives, 71; Scilly Islands, 20, 48, 49; Sennen, 45; Shuffley, 63; Sithney and Breage, 23; Snuffboxes, 22; Tragedies of, 11, 15; Troon, 68; Wool, 19.
Spanish Wars, 156
Spies, 71
Steamers Hill, 14
"Stems," 172–3
Stone, Harris, 173
Sunday Observance, 142 et seq., 195

Tailor's apprentices, 67
Tehidy, 80
Three-mile limit, 210
"Tow-boat," 172
Trawling, 184, 193, 195, 200, 205, 208 et seq.
Trawl nets, 193–209
Tregosse, Thomas, 143
Trengrouse, Henry, 102 note, 121 note, 123 et seq.
Triggs, William, 120
Troutbeck, Parson, 87
"Tucking," 152, 175
Turkish pirates, 157–8
Tywarnhayle, 80

Walker, Commodore, 99
Wardour Castle, 83
West Indies, 168
Whitley, H. M., 83 note
William le Poer, 79
Winnianton, 80
Wreckers: 30, 85, 102 et seq., 109; English coasts, 107;

INDEX

Gentry as, 79, 80, 82, 84, 85; Mounts Bay, 114; Tinners as, 88–90, 92, 100, 101

Wrecking: Bedruthan Steps, 116, 118; Breage, 87; Dangers of, 102, 104; Germoe, 87; Godrevy, 104: Gunwalloe, 81, 91, 102; Letters concerning, 89–90; Looe, 92; Mount's Bay, 113–15; Perranzabuloe, 91; Porthleven, 84, 92, 102, 103; The Lizard, 77, 85; St. Merryn, 110; Scilly Islands, 79, 86, 87; Sennen, 105

Wrecks: *Alcida*, 91; *Anson*, 121, 124; *Association*, 94; *Boscawen*, 99; the "coffee-wreck," 116; *Eagle*, 94; *Firebrand*, 94; *Good Samaritan*, 116 et seq.; *James Alexander*, 109; *Lady Lucy*, 91; *Les Landois*, 105; *Mary*, 104; *North Britain*, 131; "Prince Charles' Wardrobe," 81; *Resolution*, 102; *Romney*, 94; *St. Andrew*, 81; *Suffolk*, 119; the "tea-wreck," 116; *Thames*, 127; *Vigilante*, 91

Wrecks, number of, 105

"Yawlers," 189–92

Lightning Source UK Ltd.
Milton Keynes UK
UKOW05f2223201213

223485UK00001B/155/P